Bible FU...

SEASONAL
PAGEANTS
and Skits

SONG
SHEETS
INCLUDED!

WRITTEN BY

Susan Parsons

Edited by: Lois Keffer
Cover Design: Granite Design
Interior Design: Dana Sherrer, iDesignEtc.
Photography: Susan Parsons
Models: Julie Fleck, De Shawn Gemmen, Rachael Gemmen, Simon Gemmen, Aurora Parsons, Allison Smith, Joshua Smith, Nicholas Phifer

Printed in the United States

First printing, 2003
1 2 3 4 5 6 7 8 9 10 08 07 06 05 04 03

ISBN: 0781439604

TABLE OF CONTENTS

PART THREE: Stagecraft and Special Effects

INTRODUCTION

Pageants and plays can set the stage for some of the best church experiences your kids will ever have. All of us remember the thrill of wearing angel wings or a shepherd's beard at Christmas time! You were happily waiting "backstage" in a Sunday school room, trying out your angel wings from chair to floor, and somewhere there was a director with an elevated heart rate whose only solace was that the show was almost over!

Take delight in guiding children through these special events, knowing that these moments will stand out in the minds of your young actors. Not only will children remember the roles they played, but the experience of presenting a pageant will teach its own invaluable lessons about celebration, teamwork and honoring God.

And let's not forget what kind of experience we want you to have as the director! The church dramas you've worked on in the past may have fried your nerves and left you frazzled and frustrated. Some of my friends have found that the mental and physical demands of producing pageants spoiled the blessed Christmas season. And that's exactly why I wrote this book—to help you learn the ropes of smooth-running productions and actually enjoy doing it!

Pageants and plays don't have to be life-altering events for you as the director. But they can be life-altering events—in the best way—for the kids you lead. You don't have to put on a Broadway-scale production to edify the audience and give the kids a meaningful church and theater experience. This book will help you present wonderful pageants and plays on a scale you can handle. Kids will grow spiritually and emotionally as they work together on productions that touch the hearts of your whole congregation. There's nothing that builds esteem like a job well done and well appreciated! So get ready to see how pageants and plays can become the experiences you've always dreamed they could be.

Susan Parsons

THE COUNTDOWN BEGINS

The clock is ticking!

Perhaps you've found yourself in this situation. It's December 1 and the pastor has just informed you that he's looking forward to your kids' Christmas program in "big church" on the Sunday before Christmas. First, you deal with the frustration that this is the first time anyone's remembered to *ask* you about a pageant. Second, you get scared because you only have a couple of weeks. And third, you grab this book and find hope! Yes, there is hope! You can do it, and the kids can enjoy it. And best of all, God will be glorified.

The program you select will depend upon the lead time you've been given. If you just have a couple of weeks, you may only have time to teach the children a Christmas carol or two and gather up some costumes with the help of church moms and dads.

On the other hand, if your church begins planning as far back as September or October, you'll have plenty of time to pull together a more polished presentation. You may need to fill a 30-minute slot on Sunday morning, or even present an hour-long evening performance. Either way, don't sweat it. No matter what your situation, if you plan a production that's suitable for your time frame and resources, you can put together something that looks great, sounds great, provides a fun and valuable learning experience for the kids and inspires the audience.

CONSIDER THE LENGTH AND COMPLEXITY OF YOUR PROGRAM

The length and complexity of your program depend on two main factors: the **number in your cast** and the **time you have to prepare.** These are the variables that determine whether you should stick to

an *easy* program or try an *intermediate*
program. Notice we don't include *hard* or
advanced programs in this book. That's
because most churches reserve their more
difficult programs for multiage casts
involving the whole church, with
sophisticated technical and stage
management aspects.

For your convenience, all the programs
in this book can be performed in less than
an hour. You can enrich any of these
programs by adding "spectacle" or extra
songs or dances. If you have the energy and
resources, go for it!

QUICK AND EASY PROGRAMS

Quick and easy programs can be performed
by 20 children or less, on a tight schedule
and limited budget. They consist of a single,
clear theme, and they require a minimum
number of children to memorize lines.

You accomplish quick and easy
programs with narration, a bit of spectacle
and song. Rehearsals will consist of
rehearsing simple songs, and learning
where to stand for the presentation. The
narrator may be a person of any age. A
child who reads well and with expression
would make a wonderful narrator.
However, it's usually less of a hassle to find
a willing adult do the job of reading lines
that link the songs together.

How do you make a "spectacle"? With
costumes, banners or other props. Kids may
wear hats and hold objects relevant to the
message of the song and theme. If you
have a few good readers, you can attach
cards bearing Scripture verses to props so
the reading is a little less obvious.

INTERMEDIATE PROGRAMS

The next level of programming involves
more individual participation—more
"roles" for kids. Individual parts make for
more challenging directing because you'll
need to work with each child on
memorization and positioning (blocking).
But the payoff is worth it as you add depth
with plot and characterization and give
each child a moment in the spotlight.

You can simplify the intermediate programs in this book by combining character parts or using some kids in multiple roles. The multiple role adjustment usually requires time for a costume change. Kids who struggle with memorizing lines can have them written on note cards attached to props.

What Do You Have to Work With?

Every church has its own potential as well as limiting factors. The key is simply to choose a program that fits your resources.

These are the assets you'll need to evaluate:

1. available talent
2. financial resources
3. staging capacity
4. props and costumes

If you have lots of resources at your disposal, use them! If your situation calls for a more modest production, know that your young actors' and singers' efforts will still bring great joy to their audience. A small, well done production will be a much happier experience for everyone than an extravaganza fraught with flaws.

Available Talent

While you don't want to make self-centered "stars" of talented kids in your group, it is important to recognize gifts that God has given your little ones and to offer a place for them to develop.

Whether you have five kids in your group or 150, you will find varying levels of creative ability among them. You may have one child with a remarkable singing voice. If so, your program should offer a place for that gift. Perhaps you could let the child sing a solo verse before the chorus chimes in. This gives your soloist confidence in using his or her gift for God and allows the audience to enjoy a budding talent.

Other children in your group may be superb readers. Use their expressive voices as narrators. Still other children may excel in dance or gymnastics. These skills can be put to wonderful use in a celebratory processional in larger productions— tumblers coming down the aisles doing handsprings and flips always grab the attention of audiences and lend an air of celebration as the program opens. Just behind them can come little boys marching in with flags and banners in Jesus' honor; little girls in white robes and floral crowns can wave streamers or palm branches in praise to God! What a way to open a play or a concert!

Financial Resources

A budget for children's productions? This may be a foreign concept to your church.

Take heart—you're not alone. Many churches don't have the luxury of funds to spend on a pageant or play, but they still want to offer pageant experiences to their children and audiences.

If you do have a budget, count your blessings and consider the purchases you might make.

1. CDs, printed music

2. props

3. sets

4. costumes

5. honorariums for skilled helpers

CDs, printed music

Kids learn music so quickly when they can hear it and sing along. And a variety of musical styles keeps them interested. Though taping and photocopying is a tempting shortcut, it shortchanges dedicated Christian artists who earn their living with their creative gifts. Adding new music to your repertoire is always a good investment!

Props

"Props" (short for "properties") are the physical items you need in a play to help convey realism. Properties in a typical Christmas program may include shepherd staffs, a manger, a doll, hay, etc.

The props that you use in your play can be elaborate or simple. Since props are seen from a distance and get handled by children, creating "faux" pieces from foam or plywood is often your best bet. A listing in your church bulletin will often bring forth just the prop you're looking for, but be careful not to have kids use antiques unless they're sturdy.

Some shows use no props at all, but allow the audience to use their imaginations to "see" things that are not there. Mimes are particularly effective at getting the audience to use imagination instead of sight. But miming takes great acting skill, and most children aren't there yet. You're usually better off with real props.

Occasionally a particular script will call for a special prop that "makes" the production—a star that lights up on cue at Christmas, a pulley and harness that allows an angel to "fly," a smoke machine, an eye-catching set that lends needed atmosphere, or even a spotlight. These little investments can increase your repertoire for the future as well.

Sets

Backgrounds add a wonderful touch of realism to a play and make kids feel really professional! You might just have someone in your congregation who loves to build and another person who paints and decorates.

If you don't have room in your stage area for plywood sets, consider painting the background on sheets and hanging them. Airbrush is a wonderful medium for this. You'll find helps for set design and construction in Part Three.

Costumes

Your costume closet is a resource you'll turn to again and again. Basic Bibletime costumes are simple to make. Talented seamstresses in your congregation may be willing to tackle more challenging projects if you provide patterns and material. Costume rental is also an option for more elaborate outfits.

Excellent online resources offer a variety of patterns. Type "costumes" into your favorite search engine and you're likely to find exactly what you're looking for within just a few seconds. Chapter Three gives detailed instructions and photos for several basic costumes.

Honorariums

Consider using part of your budget to pay a modest fee to volunteers who sew costumes and build and paint sets. Some folks make the false assumption that a person who accepts pay for such work is "unspiritual." Remember 1 Timothy 5:18: "For the Scripture says, …'The worker deserves his wages.'" There are those who may want to donate their time *pro bono*. For others, volunteering time may put a squeeze on other essential needs. Use discretion as you decide whether or not to offer a small honorarium.

Make a Spectacle!

Think about spectacle for a moment. Look at the word and think of spectacles like the little glasses worn by Benjamin Franklin. Those spectacles allowed Franklin to see. And "spectacle" in theater helps the audience "see" more than what is actually there. These visual effects are always fun for audiences. In the future, you may even incorporate the use of additional spectacle devices such as smoke machines, special lighting and the use of scrims and screens and multi-media. Once you master the things in this book, you may choose to venture off into the realm of special effects, which is a realm set aside for the "truly called!" If you love theater, you will love, and pursue, special effects!

This book will suggest ways to use certain special effects. And don't be afraid—they are not always expensive, nor are they difficult to use. Throw them in where you can and your audience will be wowed by the results! A little showmanship will excite your audience and your kids. Remember that the more you can keep your audience's attention, the more chance you have of delivering the message of Christ, straight to their hearts! Look for special effects ideas in Part Three.

THE POWER OF STORY

Stories slip right past our Western tendencies to dissect and analyze. Those who witnessed God's story played out on the stage of history lived and breathed life-changing moments of God's power at work. We weren't there. But we can go there and take others on the journey through the marvelous vehicles of story, stage and spectacle.

As you step into the role of producer/director, you're stepping into God's story on many levels in your own life as well as the lives of your children and their audiences. And when people experience God's story, God continues to move through lives, through history.

Deuteronomy 32:7 exhorts us, "Remember the days of old; consider the generations long past. Ask your father and he will tell you, your elders, and they will explain to you."

We make this effort so we can tell God's story in a unique way that touches many lives and leaves a unique and lasting impression. And that's why we can ask God to bless our efforts, and why he does so, over and over!

THE BOTTOM LINE

Here's what to take away from this chapter: No matter whether your resources are abundant or meager, you have enough to minister effectively through drama and pageants! You have enough, because that's all you have. God doesn't expect you to fail; he expects you to succeed with the "five small stones" at your disposal.

Keep in mind that your objective is to encourage both the participants and audience in their walk with Christ. Approach your programs with the expectation that God will supply everything you need to be spiritually effective; then rely on him to do just that. Communicate this to your kids. Begin and end rehearsals with prayer. Keep before them the clear objective of glorifying God and watch how that brings out their best!

DEALING WITH FEELINGS

Creative people are just full of ideas. That's what's wonderful about getting a team together to coordinate your production. Sometimes those ideas can go in vastly different directions. From the get-go you need to keep your vision before you and clearly define leadership roles.

What's your vision for a particular production? Think it through carefully before your team meets. Open with that vision. How might God use this program to build his kingdom? When you brainstorm, listen to everyone's ideas. Then focus and agree on a course of action based on

1. what best fulfills the vision,
2. what works with your resources and
3. what you've learned from past successes and failures.

Something that sounds great at the brainstorming table may turn out to be just that—great! But you may have tried a similar idea last year and it didn't work out. Past experiences tempered with fresh enthusiasm can guide your creative team in the right direction.

If you need to turn down an idea that someone is excited about, you can handle the situation graciously by saying, "You know, I really like that idea. I'm not sure it's what we want to do in this production, but let's keep it on the back burner. It might be just the right thing for next year."

Open your meetings with prayer and ask God to help bring the best ideas forward and keep egos out of the way. Seek a gentle and appropriate way to set priorities and expectations for everyone involved.

NO-TEAR AUDITIONS

Try-outs and casting for pageants and plays bring out the best and worst in people. The potential for emotional moments is significant. Kids celebrate or cry because they did or didn't get a certain role; budding "stage moms" may push to get their little ones front and center; workers may have creative disagreements that result in tension and hurt feelings. All in an effort to glorify God! You can avoid these emotional pitfalls by having a few strategies in place as you begin.

The terms "auditions" or "try-outs" are misnomers in church drama. An audition should be simply a way of getting your volunteers to come together and offer their talents. Never let it be a way of eliminating children! Jesus spoke of welcoming the children to impatient disciples who wanted to turn them away. Let his words be your guide: "Let the children come!" Find a place in the choir or in a flag corps or as a props assistant for every child who comes to audition.

Guard your heart against seeing any child as a "misfit," and avoid clumping such "overflow" children together. Think beyond the theatrical quality of your production. Consider feelings and the growing faith of little ones—children whose first concepts of God are molded in part by the church they attend. Let the Holy Spirit guide you as you select your cast. Use your auditions as a means to get to know what kids' talents are and where they could be used and developed.

In your Christmas pageant, lots of little girls will want to play Mary and no one else, and lots of boys will want to be the wicked King Herod and nothing but King Herod. In other programs, kids will want to play the leading roles or the roles with the coolest costumes. Unfortunately, there can only be one child per role. This means someone likely will be disappointed.

If this becomes a problem in your group, you might consider having two performances in which you have two different casts, at least for the lead roles. Some complexities come up if you go this route. For example, consider whether you'll have two costumes per role, or whether your cast members can wear the same size. It's always a good idea to have understudies for key roles. You never know when chickenpox will strike—or laryngitis!

There are other ways to deal with the sorrows of not getting "the lead" or the desired role. On one hand, it's a life lesson that every child will learn at some time and it may be a good thing to get it over with. On the other hand, you want to offset the discomfort as much as possible. One way is to be sure that you stress the importance of every role so that kids will want to play them all!

You may have kids come to an audition with no ability to act, carry off choreography or carry a tune. But perhaps they can still lend a smile to the choir or carry a handsome satin banner proclaiming the majesty of Jesus! Props managers are invaluable, and so are prompters. There's always something that a child can do in a program. If all else fails, invent a small role. And take extra pains to make their costumes or props special. Keep in mind how important this church experience can be for every child. It reflects the love of the church, which reflects the love and acceptance of God.

Figure 1

Some kids want to do choreography so they can wear colorful costumes. Others want to be angels so they can wear wings for a day. This is true for most kids—cool costumes are a real draw. So just make sure your banner bearers and flag wavers have costumes and make-up, just like Mary, Joseph, dancers, shepherds and angels. And why should your kids' choir have to wear white tops and blue skirts or trousers? Let them dress in Bibletime costumes too! It will add to the spectacle. And if it's not a Christmas or Easter program, simple robes made from sheets of the same dye lot (keep in mind that different fabrics may absorb color differently) or inexpensive fabric can help unify your group and help them sense how special the production really is. Keep

in mind that you can use the robes over and over for future performances, unless the children purchase their own costumes.

Be sensitive to gender roles. When there's a shortage of boys, some girls won't mind playing wise men or shepherds in your Christmas play, especially if their friends will also be wise men or shepherds. Girls can be disguised easily with beards and mustaches (see figure 1). But others may feel uncomfortable in an out-of-gender role. My first role in a play was that of a shepherd in a Christmas pageant at an old storefront church in downtown Detroit, Michigan, circa 1961. While I liked being able to perform, I felt awkward playing the part of a boy. I can still remember wanting to wear angel wings and a pretty halo instead. My mixed feelings and half-smile

Figure 2

were captured on camera for posterity (see figure 2)!

Today, my own 10-year-old daughter doesn't give a second thought to playing a shepherd or wise man if called upon to do so. Times sure have changed!

Other children in your group may enjoy helping with the set painting and building. If there is a way you can use these gifts, do so! If kids don't find self-worth in the Body of Christ, they will seek it elsewhere, so be especially vigilant to try to plug kids in. And remind each child that his or her particular gift is vitally important. The kids who pass out flyers and programs are your little marketers and they, too, are incredibly important. Recruit children who will pledge to pray that the program will touch someone's heart. Let them know that without the spiritual result that they are praying for, the performers are little more than clanging noisemakers and glittery spectacles—like sparks on wet pavement, they sizzle and disappear.

Dealing With Stage Parents

You've probably heard the term "stage mother" before. It's a term given to moms who push their kids into performance situations, largely for their own satisfaction instead of the children's. Stage mothers and fathers tend to direct their own children during rehearsals. "Smile, Mary Jane! You look dead up there!"

Stage parents also tend to direct the director where their kids are concerned, and this can sorely try your ability to be longsuffering, especially when you're under stress. "You can't even see Bradley in the back where you put him! Can't you move him to the front? And Lisa shouldn't wear lavender—redheads should never wear lavender. You should make her costume a nice teal color to bring out her features…." Now what do you do with someone like that?

Think prevention! Make over-zealous parents a non-issue by designating a seating area for them that's set well back from the stage. Hang a decorative sign that says "Parents' Section. Thanks for your help and support!" You may want to have a helper or older child escort parents there. The physical distance you've set between the parents and the action will give a big clue that you appreciate their support as silent observers.

If a stage mom still gives unwelcome input, your goal is to keep the direction of the play firmly in hand without creating discord. Recognize that this situation has a strong spiritual aspect, and ask the Holy Spirit to season your words and reactions.

Be secure and calm (not cold) and say something that will validate her concerns, if indeed they are valid. Only make changes that are doable and truly enhance the production. You can say something like, "Thank you so much for pointing that out. I'll make every effort to make sure every child can be seen. But as for Lisa's costume, I'm so sorry—we chose the colors for the way they'd look as a group. I'm sure some really good stage makeup will do the trick. Would you like to help?"

You might just recruit another worker this way!

Your Contagious Spirit

If you approach your productions with

1. a spirit of joy,

2. an enthusiastic determination to bring out the best in everyone and

3. a focus on glorifying God,

you'll find that you're attitude is contagious! Everyone around you will be infected with your positive spirit. It will spill over on your kids and your audience.

As you prepare for your production, ask God to give you a warm, winsome spirit. Bathe the relationships in prayer. Invite God to be in the details, and you won't be disappointed.

Debriefing

Believe it or not, when the show is over you may experience a let-down. Your mind and body have been devoted to getting the program up and running; then, in a single night or day, it's over. It's kind of like slamming on the brakes at 60 mph—the car might stop, but you keep going! Ouch!

While you're bound to be tired and relieved to be done with all the rehearsals and preparation, schedule one more meeting—a de-briefing with all your workers. Have it no more than a week after the production. And make it fun! Order pizza, have a potluck, or reserve a section at a restaurant. The church may be able to pick up the check. If not, choose a restaurant that all your team members will be able to afford.

Get together for some fun, and talk about the program—the challenges, the blessings, the way God intervened, the funny times, the moving times. These processing questions will help everyone draw important lessons from your experience together so that your next production will benefit.

DEBRieFinG OUR PROGRam

1. What was your favorite part of putting on this production?

_____

2. What was the most challenging part for you?

_____

3. What would you do differently?

_____

4. In what ways did you see God intervene?

_____

5. What particular blessings did you receive through this program—through preparation or performance?

_____

6. What can we do better next time?

_____

7. What changes did you see in kids as the program developed?

_____

8. What was the greatest personal lesson you'll take away from this production?

_____

Got Help?

Feel like you're flying solo? That can be a little scary, especially as the program date approaches and you see announcements popping up in church bulletins and newsletters.

Remember Moses' hesitation to take on an enormous job? It went something like this: "Here am I. Send my brother." God gave Moses a staff as well as a helpful brother and sister. Later, when Moses' outstretched arms grew tired, Aaron and Hur became his literal support group! And Joshua handled the front lines, watching for Moses' signal. Each of these people played key roles in Israel's victory, with God's help, of course.

You may be the Moses in this program. You may know how the whole shebang should be run; you may have experience that others do not have; but you only have two hands and one mouth. You could hammer, sew, glue, paint and direct around

the clock and still end up short. Instead, start looking around and praying for God to point out your Aarons, Miriams, Hurs and Joshuas. Make your life simpler—delegate!

For starters, you can delegate the tasks of set design and construction, costuming and music direction. You can delegate as much as you need to. You'll probably want to hang onto some of the tasks you really enjoy and for which God has gifted you—*if* you have time.

Maybe you're good at everything from script writing to building sets and sewing costumes. Even so, you'll do a better job and enjoy it more if you share those responsibilities with others. Besides, you don't want to deprive anyone of the great experience of getting involved in children's programs!

As you develop your program, it's easy to slip into "control freak" mode. Some really creative types require a major crisis to get them off the control wagon and start handing out responsibility. So think of it this way: besides ministering to the kids in your cast and the audience who will hear them, preparing your program gives you an opportunity to disciple your helpers and crew. You may help some talented folks in your congregation discover the joy of using their God-given gifts in his service.

If it's your vision that's driving the program, there's no doubt that it's hard to surrender that vision to the creativity of others. *"But it's my baby…."* As you tackle the difficult task of empowering others, think about what you have to gain! As God works in your heart and the hearts of your helpers, the creativity of his Spirit is unleashed. When the Body of Christ works in harmony, the blessings increase exponentially.

Here's a list of responsibilities you can think about sharing with gifted people in your congregation:

- Script development
- Directing rehearsals
- Music/accompaniment
- Managing kids
- Costumes and props
- Makeup
- Set design
- Sound
- Publicity

SCRiPT DEVELOPMENT

You'll find some great scripts in this book. But when you need a script for a specific occasion that's not covered here, or when inspiration hits in the middle of the night, don't feel limited by what's already in print. Jot down your ideas and start thinking about possible writers. Is there someone who writes a really great column for your church newsletter? Do you know a clever person who is full of quips and silly things that make kids giggle? How about a gifted teenager who shows some flair for writing? There are many more aspiring writers in the world than there are published ones. Ask God to help you find one!

Show your writing apprentice the play formats in this book, share your vision and give lots of assurance that this won't be a solo project. Do this weeks, even months, before the rest of the team is on board. Plan to meet, perhaps with a larger creative team, to go over the rough draft your writer produces. Explain up front that there will be a tweaking process. You might just find a great talent who will be a valuable resource to you for years to come!

DiRECTiNG REHEARSALS

Rehearsals usually turn out to be both fun and chaotic. Even though you may be a marvelous director, someone with that gift and vision needs to be able to stand back and take in the big picture. So find yourself an assistant director—someone who can get the kids excited about their lines and can manage them as a group. What does that leave for you to do? Delegate, collaborate, inspire!

You'll want to avoid the role of back-seat driver for tasks you've delegated. Assistant directors need the freedom to use their own creativity and sense of chemistry with the cast. Think long and hard before you decide to redirect. Ask yourself, "Is this my own pet idea, or is the other way just as good?" Don't assert your idea unless you're quite convinced it's necessary to maintain the quality of the production.

If you decide it's best to do a little redirecting, use a tactful approach that keeps your assistant director's authority intact.

- Make notes and discuss your suggestion after the rehearsal, not in front of the kids.
- Say, "Things went well tonight. You do a terrific job of handling the kids. I have an idea that might enhance the production even more. What would you think of…?"

Have your cast give the assistant director an appreciative round of applause at the end of each rehearsal. And give him or her big-time billing in your credits!

MUSIC/ACCOMPANIMENT

If you're using music in your program, decide whether to use live or recorded accompaniment. While recorded accompaniment tracks give you big, sophisticated sound, live accompaniment has the strong advantage of being able to flex with whatever happens when you're live on stage.

Don't assume your church music director or pianist will have time to rehearse with you and play for the performance. Music personnel invest a lot of time in practice for their own performances as well as with choirs, soloists and ensembles. You may be able to find a less busy accompanist in your congregation who would love the opportunity to serve in this way. Don't forget about guitarists. Acoustic guitar can add a lovely touch to some plays. And electric guitar makes kids feel all grown up and groovy!

If you find yourself short on accompaniment options, you can ask an accomplished musician to make a tape for you to use in rehearsal. Then you'll need an accompaniast live only for the dress rehearsal and performance.

Managing Kids

If you have lots of kids in your program (or more than nine per supervising adult), you'll need some assistance in corralling them. You may call upon parents, college students or other responsible adults to help keep the kids focused and attentive.

A rule of thumb is this: you need **at least** one adult for every seven kids in your group to "herd" kids where they need to be, coach them to stay quiet and alert while you're rehearsing an actor or another group, praise kids for their effort, and remind them what they're doing and why. Helpers listen to what the director is saying and affirm it all with nods and smiles in an effort to "bring the kids in."

When kids need a little individual coaching, you'll want a helper right there to prompt and encourage. And, of course, there are the inevitable potty breaks. Getting kids quickly to the restroom and back to rehearsal is a service you'll be glad to have someone perform.

Costumes, Makeup and Props

You'll need people to help make costumes, obtain and apply makeup and collect props. Parents may be your best resource in these areas. For your peace of mind and theirs, plan to have everything ready and in place a week before the program. Keep all your supplies secured in a safe, designated area until production time.

Set Design

Set design is a luxury, but it's great if you can afford it. Besides creating sets, you'll need to think about where to store them. If you have space, go for it! You can do a lot with backgrounds painted on sheets suspended from the ceiling and taped to the floor. Sheets have the advantage of not causing injury if they're accidentally knocked over.

Your set people don't have to be great with kids, since their work is done apart from rehearsals. Teenagers and college students who are into art may be a great resource for designing, building and painting backdrops. You'll also want to enlist someone with a large van or truck to collect potted palms and fig trees to give your sets a touch of nature.

For a nativity play, your set can range from a couple of plants and a manger on your platform to a stable built of wood. If you have a good painter on hand, a Bethlehem backdrop painted on several theatre flats is a wonderful idea.

Sound

Good sound management is essential. If

your children's words cannot be heard, the program will fall flat and everyone will be disappointed. Children need microphones to be heard, but some kids are shy around them. For this reason, spend a bit of time letting each child learn to step up to the microphone and speak, without touching it, yelling into it or turning away from it. This is a lesson in discipline and all kids should have a good time learning how to use it. Be sure to tell the shy kids how wonderful and strong their voices sound when they use the microphone correctly.

You might want to put wireless lapel mikes on main characters in a play. Kids will need to learn the dos and don'ts of wearing these mikes and practice with them a couple of times before your production. Getting kids "rigged up" requires patience as well as technical know-how.

You will need a dependable technical person to run your tape or CD player if you use prerecorded accompaniment. That person will also need to adjust microphone

Figure 33: The backdrop for this multi-age pageant was made of 10-foot cardboard sheets donated by a packaging company. The sheets were cut to fit the back wall (right up to the high ceiling!), duct-taped together and painted. In the dark blue sky, holes were punched and white Christmas lights were inserted to form stars! It was a beautiful effect!

levels at a soundboard. If your church has an audio/visual person, go to that person first to describe your needs. Work within your church's existing experts.

People who regularly handle sound at your church will be thankful if your sound person jots down all control settings left by the previous engineer. This will allow the church sound to be put back to normal following your production. Actually, there should be few (if any) changes to the existing levels, other than microphone and tape playback volume.

Your sound volunteers may do double duty with lights and spots as well as fog machines, sound effects and any other technical treats you plan for your production.

PUBLiCiTY

Publicity gets kids excited about what's coming. It also gives them a helpful little reality check about learning their parts and getting to rehearsals.

For most children's productions, church bulletins and newsletters are the main publicity vehicles. Consider having someone talented with lettering create a special title treatment for your show that can be scanned and included with each announcement. Your artist might even be a child. There's something wonderfully appealing about children's art!

If your church uses an LCD projector for song lyrics or announcements, your publicity person can see that a slide about your production gets included. Adding digital photos of the kids involved will bring ooh and ahs from participants and their parents.

Delegating responsibility will keep your sanity intact and allow you to focus on making your production a spiritually positive event for everyone. It doesn't hurt to begin to drop feelers months in advance, so when showtime approaches you have a good idea of those who might be willing to be involved. A little "soft sell" ahead of time is a lot easier than cold calling when you're just a few weeks out. Keep your eyes peeled and chat with folks along the way. When the time comes, you'll have smooth sailing.

GROWING YOUR COSTUME COLLECTION

To kids, costumes are more than half the fun of putting on a pageant! Costumes may be as elaborate as velvet and satin, or as simple as a paper hat. Whatever you can afford in terms of money, time and effort will be enough. Don't feel pressured to do any more, but don't shrink back and do less than you can. Whatever you do, do it as unto the Lord, to capture the most attention and subsequently plant God's message.

This chapter gives ideas to help you be a good steward financially, while providing your cast with costumes that will inspire and excite them to do well. You'll find detailed instructions for:

- Basic Bibletime Robes
- Shepherds
- Wise Men and Kings
- Bibletime Women
- Bibletime Children
- Beards and Mustaches
- Pilgrim hats and collars
- Patriotic hats
- Angels
- Star
- Animals
- Makeup

If you use satin, taffeta, lamé, or certain other shiny fabrics, you'll notice a tendency for cut edges to fray to the point of becoming cobwebs. You can offset this at least three ways:

Use Fray Check™, Fabri-Tac™ or some other anti-fray product after cutting the pattern. This liquid comes in little plastic bottles. Apply it to the fraying edge of the fabric. It "glues" fraying threads together and keeps them from coming apart (see fig. 3).

Use a "zig-zag" stitch on your machine. Bind the edges by stitching as close to the edge as possible—even slightly going over the edge.

Fold the edge over about 1/4 inch and stitch it in place with a straight stitch.

Before you dive into the how-to's, remember that you do not have to be an experienced

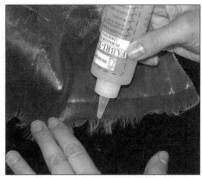
Figure 3

seamstress or craftsman to make these costumes. It helps to know how to thread a sewing machine and run a straight stitch. Beyond that, you don't have to know much! (Trust me—I didn't!) And don't try too hard to be neat. Nobody will ever see your crooked stitches!

First, be encouraged! Bibletime costumes are simpler to create than you might imagine. With basic tunics and a few accessory changes, you can give quite a realistic impression of Bibletime garb.

Bible folk wore lots of different types of clothing—long tunics, short tunics, robes, veils and sometimes no more than loincloths. (Of course, you're not going to resort to loincloths, although admittedly, they would save you money on fabric!)

Male Bibletime Dress

The most versatile Bibletime outfits consist of a long tunic with bell sleeves, covered by a robe called an aba. This outer robe is sort of a caftan with an open front. You don't have to have this layered look for your

programs—unless you choose to and have the time and money to make them. You may just use an under-tunic with a sash and leave it at that.

Here's an easy way to make the basic under-tunic—the basic "T." Use solid colored or striped old sheets (no florals!) or other fabric cut into modified "T" shapes. Lay the fabric out in a double layer with the fold at the top. Measure the "T" top to

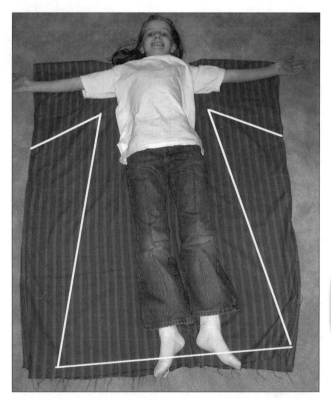
Figure 4

match the breadth of the child's outstretched arms (fig. 4) either to the wrists or elbows. Measure the length from the child's shoulders to the floor. Keep in mind that a belt will shorten it somewhat.

The garment length should take on an "A" or bell shape as shown in figure 4. Stitch the side seams and hem the bottom edge (if you have time) to make a great Bibletime garment! (See fig. 5.) You may need to make a slit at the neck that extends a few inches down toward the breastbone area to allow the head to slip through easily. If you

Figure 5

like, you can punch a few holes on the sides of this slit and loosely run a shoelace through. Use a rope or fabric scraps for a belt. Add a contrasting remnant fabric for the headpiece (fringe is an option on this piece) and tie it on with a headband or fabric scrap, and you've got a Bibletime

● For kids approximately four feet six inches tall (under 10 years old, or younger than fifth grade), two yards of fabric is enough for the T-robe. For tall kids, get 2-1/2 yards and you should be fine. Fold the fabric in half width-wise and cut the robe with the top and bottom running across the width of the fabric (the longer direction). The sleeves may not come to the wrists, which is fine.

character! If you have a bit of time, save your fabric scraps from the tunics and rip strips about 2-inches wide and three feet long or more. Braid the strips to create interesting belts! Use different patterns for each strip and you'll be amazed at the beautiful ropes you can create!

The caftan over-tunic costumes are super-easy to make. They are simply two rectangular fabric pieces sewn together, with an open bottom, and openings left for the head and hands. Make the length of the caftan several inches shorter than the tunic so that the tunic shows underneath. Cut the center front of the caftan so it remains open and loose with the belted tunic underneath.

SHEPHERDS

For shepherds, the length of the tunic should be shorter— falling just below the knee—with a nubby caftan over it. The more rustic-looking the fabric,

Figure 6

the better. For the caftan you can use faux fur or fleece, or even burlap if it's not too scratchy! Stay with drab or natural colors. Use a broom handle or stick for the shepherd's staff.

WISe MeN AND KINGS

Other Bibletime characters, such as the Magi, may warrant shiny or colorful fabrics.

Figure 7

Don't be afraid that you'll have to buy high-priced satins and velvets. You may be surprised at how inexpensive some glitzy fabrics are. Shiny or metallic lamé is relatively affordable and makes terrific costumes for wise men or angels. Instead of velvet, use inexpensive velour. You can make the basic tunic out of one of these materials and add a shiny gold belt. Rummage through remnant piles to find short lengths of contrast material for belts and turbans.

Turbans are expected for the Magi—and there are several ways to make them. One easy way is to make a narrow "tube" out of a satiny or colorful fabric. Stuff the tube with fiberfill and stitch the ends together to form a ring that fits around the head. Tie a ribbon around the stitched area, and glue the knot in place on the inside of the ring. Tie ribbons in this way all around the ring—every two inches or so. Decorate the front of the ring with a fake jewel or a sparkly brooch—thrift stores have lots of gaudy pins and such, and grandma might have some lying around, too. You may decorate your turban in a variety of ways. Add a veil that goes around the sides and back (stitch or glue it to the inside of the ring). (See fig. 7.) Add an ostrich feather in the front (again, attach it to the inside of the ring).

You can vary your "tube" design. For example, instead of a tube ring, make a cylindrical turban by covering quilt batting with the fabric. Tie a string or ribbon tightly at the stitch site to form the front. Add jewels to the spot with an ostrich feather behind. Cover the top of the turban with the same kind of fabric. It's elegant!

scepTeRs

Scepters for kings are lots of fun to make and look at!

You'll need:

- A wooden dowel about 1/2-inch in diameter and a couple of feet long
- A Styrofoam® ball (2 inches in diameter)

- E-6000 epoxy paste (plastic parts will resist hot glue)
- Cap from dishwashing liquid
- Gold paint
- Sequins and fake gems

Figure 8

Carefully poke one end of the dowel an inch into the ball. Remove the dowel, fill the hole with E-6000 paste and replace the dowel. Next, take the cap from an old dishwashing liquid bottle (the kind that you pull open and push shut). Use the E-6000 to affix this cap to the top of the Styrofoam® ball. Now paint the whole thing gold. If you'd like, paint the ball in gold glitter paint. Pin or glue "jewels" (sequins and rhinestones) all over the ball. So kingly (fig. 8)!

BiBLeTiMe WoMen

The under-tunics of Bible time women were often short-sleeved—and nearly sleeveless, though not

Figure 9

quite (fig. 9). A robe with bell-sleeves was often worn over this. Unlike men, Jewish women always wore head coverings. The head covering is simply a long strip of fabric draped shawl-like over the head, crossed in front of the neck and flipped over the shoulders. It was important that the women's hair was covered. For this reason, women often braided their hair in the back to keep it from falling on their shoulders.

Make these costumes attractive by using contrasting colors. A natural linen color simulates flax for the under-tunic. Use soft, solid colors for the robes and shawls. Again, the remnant pile can be a treasure trove for smaller pieces such as shawls and belts.

BiBLeTiMe CHiLDRen

Bible time children don't require headwear, although school-age boys may wear yarmulkes—the small skullcap that covers the crown of the head (fig. 10). You can make them easily by cutting a seven-inch circle out of dark felt. Fold the circle in half

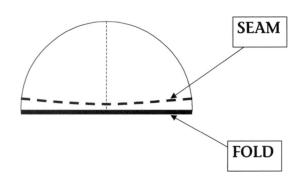

SEAM

FOLD

and stitch a seam on the fold that creates a very slight curve.

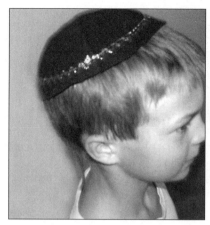
Figure 10

Open the circle, fold it in half the other way (still seam side out) and stitch another curved seam. These seams will draw the circle into a slight cup to fit the head.

Figure 11

Decorate the outside with some shiny rickrack stitched an inch from the brim.

Little girls don't wear yarmulkes. They may have long hair or wear a kerchief over their hair and tie it behind the neck (fig. 11).

Beards and Mustaches

Beards are easy to make. Of course, you can always draw them on with eyebrow pencils. But if you have access to some old wigs or fake fur, the beards will be more fun for the kids.

If you have old wigs (curly, gray ones are especially effective!), cut them up, "nap" flowing downward. Cut the width to

fit ear-to-ear (too narrow and you'll have a fu-manchu!). Cut the length as long as you like, keeping in mind that a beard doesn't have to touch the chest. If you cut the wig correctly, you can use the top part for a mustache by just cutting a slit for the mouth. It's important to cut on the fabric *behind* the actual hair, so you don't come up with a chopped-up wig look. You can attach elastic to the two top corners of the beard and let the child wear it over his head, under his headpiece. These can look *very* real and kids love wearing them! (See fig. 12.)

Figure 12

If you have faux fur, you can do the same thing (fig. 13), but try to keep the beards rather short or they'll look odd. As with the hair wig, cut on the fabric rather than the hair fibers, or you'll wind up with a real phony-baloney looking beard and it won't be much fun to wear or look at.

Figure 13

Animal Costumes

Animal costumes never fail to add a wonderful touch of charm and whimsy to children's productions. Sheep and lambs

Figure 14

play a prominent role in so many Bible passages because of their significance in sacrifice, atonement and the many Bibletime shepherding scenes. Other animals may come in handy in a variety of plays and skits.

Complement your animal head with plain-colored sweatpants and shirts. For example, the flock of sheep in figure 14 are wearing white turtlenecks and white sweatpants with their sheep heads. They formed the children's chorus. Not baa-d!

You can make easy (*really* easy) animal heads out of fleecy fabric using the pattern on pages 37–38 (fig. 15). It consists of only three little pieces sewn together—just two seams! You can sew two little ears right into the seam, or you can sew them on by hand or even hot-glue them on. If you use "Sherpa" fabric or thick fleece, you won't need to do any hemming at all.

The great thing about this animal head pattern is that it can be adjusted to create a variety of animal heads simply by changing the ears and trimming the hairline, or using different weights of fur or fleece. Almond-shaped (*not* triangular) three-inch ears will make an adorable lamb; small triangle ears make a cat; floppy ears create a dog; tall ears with wire stitched in makes a darling rabbit head! There's no limit to what you can do.

After you make the head caps, add makeup for the finishing touch. See the makeup section (see page 31) for details.

Angels

Angels only need a white "T" garment and a set of wings. Make wings from white wrapping tissue tied in the center and splayed out like a bow. Just pin them to the back neck area of the robe with a safety pin. Of course, you can always make

Figure 16

the old fashioned (and fun) cardboard wings, too (fig. 16). Just make sure all your angels use the same type of wings or they may be mistaken for fairies and insects!

CHOIR ROBES

Use a basic T-pattern for Angel robes. Add collars of a contrasting color (fig. 17). You can make these from large felt pieces without having to baste the edges. Cut large diamonds, then cut the centers out. Or cut circles approximately 18 inches in diameter for older elementary kids, 15 inches for younger elementary and 12 inches for preschoolers. Cut a circular hole directly in the center, between four and six inches in diameter. Then cut a slit from the inside of the circle, down about two inches. This will enable the collar to slip over the head. Position the slit in back.

Figure 17

Makeup

Makeup can serve several purposes. It can help kids' facial features show up; it can enhance animal costumes by providing whiskers, nose leather or skin color to match the animal suit; it can provide characterizing features such as mustaches and wrinkles. Best of all, it makes the show lots more fun for kids! Almost every child loves wearing face paint of some kind.

Foundation and eye makeup are not essential for kids' programs, especially if your sanctuary is very small. But if the stage may be far away for some, go ahead and use it. Lipstick, blush and mascara should simply serve to help the kids' faces "show up" at a distance. Pink lips and rosy cheeks don't look garish from far away.

If you use strong lighting, some Caucasian children can "wash out" and look very wan. A bit of powder or foundation, only slightly darker than the natural skin, will help cut back on the washout. With all complexions, a bit of blush can render a little happy color to the cheeks. Very dark-skinned children should use a bright brick, deep pink or burgundy blush instead of pastel pink or light coral. All kids will benefit from mascara—it helps their eyes show up. Some kids don't like anyone putting anything near their eyes. Do what you can, but don't push it. It's not worth the tears and smears.

Avoid sharing eye makeup or lipstick unless you use separate applicators. It's all too easy for kids to pass eye infections to each other, even if other users have no symptoms.

Boys should wear neutral shades of lipstick—don't humiliate them with puce or magenta! Nice honey-toned beiges or browns should suffice.

It's usually fairly easy to find volunteers to assist kids with makeup—it's an instant gratification project. Provide volunteers with the guidelines from this book and see how gorgeous they can make your young actors.

Figure 18

Animals

Animal faces are not just a matter of a black nose and whiskers. Notice that many animal noses are triangular—bunnies, cats, sheep. Round noses belong to dogs and bears and pigs. Use photos to guide you as you apply makeup to your kids' faces (figs. 18 and 19).

Figure 19

Uncle Sam Hats and Liberty Crowns

You can make Uncle Sam top hats two ways—easy and not so easy. Of course, the not-so-easy hat looks much better! Let your particular situation guide your choice.

Uncle Sam Top Hat #1 (more difficult)

You'll need:

- White poster board
- Red paint or red duct tape
- Blue paint
- Star template (Fig. 20)
- 11-inch plate
- 7-inch plate
- Scissors
- Tape or hot glue
- Pencil
- Yardstick

For this 3-D top hat, cut a sheet of white poster board into a rectangle about 12-inches tall and wide enough to fit around

Figure 20

the child's head. A dinner plate or pie tin works well for tracing the 11-inch circle. For a wider brim, as for the pilgrim hat pattern discussed later, use a 13-inch circle. You may use a pie tin or the lid from a frying pan. Look around your kitchen for just the right sized circle (fig. 21).

Use a pencil and a yardstick to draw a line down the length of the rectangle, four inches from the edge. Paint red stripes (or apply strips of red tape or construction paper) evenly across the wider section. Paint the four-inch section blue. Cut out six three-inch stars from white paper. Space them around the blue band and glue them. When this section dries, roll the poster board into a cylinder that will fit over the child's head (this may leave only a 1/2-inch overlap). Tape it together from the inside, or glue it with hot glue.

Next, trace a seven-inch circle (a salad plate usually works). Cut an even "+" inside this circle from edge to edge. Then, cut each quarter in half as shown (fig. 22), forming

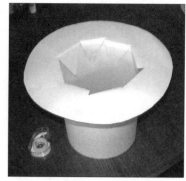
Figure 23

eight little points. Bend the points outward. Paint the circle red (the points may remain white). Place the cylinder over the circle with the points inside. Tape the points to the inside edge of the cylinder (fig. 23). You now have a hat! (See fig. 25.)

To secure the hat, punch holes in the sides and tie elastic or shoestrings from the inside to keep them on wiggly little heads.

Uncle Sam Top Hat # 2 (easy)

You'll need:

- Red, white and blue construction paper, or
- Poster board and red and blue markers or paint
- Tape or glue
- Scissors

An easier hat can be made by cutting out a one-dimensional Uncle Sam hat and taping it to the front of a poster-board or heavy construction paper headband that fits around the forehead. Make the band about two inches wide. See? I wasn't kidding when I said it was easy!

Figure 21

Figure 22

Liberty Crowns

You'll need:

- Crown pattern (fig. 24, page 40)
- Silver poster board (or white, spray-painted silver)cut to 18"x2"
- Scissors
- Adult with a craft knife or razor blade
- Stapler
- Tape
- Green-blue paint (teal—make it by adding a bit of blue to green)
- Old newspaper

Have an adult cut seven slits in the poster board with a craft knife or razor blade. Make each slit 2 1/2 inches wide, with. Leave about one inch between slits. Kids can cut seven triangles and insert them into the slits, bend the tabs against the inside of the band and secure them with tape. Then staple the ends of the crown together to fit the child's head. (The crown should be worn on the top of the head, tilted slightly backward.)

Paint your crown, let it dry, then wear it with pride! (fig. 25)

OPTION: Flashlights, covered with painted paper, make great torches. Just cut the tops of the "torches" in a zig-zag pattern and tape a crumply wad of orange cellophane with a few pointed "flames" to stick up out of the top. Turn the house lights down and let your little lights shine!

PILGRIMS' HATS, CAPS, AND COLLARS

Male Pilgrim Hat # 1 (more difficult) (Fig. 26)

You'll need:

- Poster board
- Brown and yellow paint
- Tape or hot glue
- Scissors

Figure 26

Make a pilgrim top hat similar to the Uncle Sam top hat. Roll the poster board into a cylinder. Cut four or five inches off the cylinder and roll it so that the very top is slightly tapered (but not pointed like a witch's hat!). Paint it dark brown with a bright yellow buckle in the front, just above the brim.

Figure 25

Male Pilgrim Hat # 2 (easy)

You'll need:

- Brown construction paper
- Yellow construction paper
- Poster board
- Tape or glue
- Scissors

Like the easy version of Uncle Sam's topper, all you have to do is cut out a one-dimensional hat (large enough to look real when looking straight on) and glue it to a headband that fits around the child's forehead. Make sure the pilgrim hat is slightly tapered at the top, and not quite as tall as Uncle Sam's.

Female Pilgrim Hat (Fig. 27)

You'll need:

- White poster board
- Scissors
- Stapler
- Shoestrings

Figure 27

Make a girl's cap by cutting white poster board into a rectangle, 15-1/2″ by 12″. Cut two slits in the rectangle as shown figure 28. Now, without creasing the board, draw the center flap down and pull the left flap across it (fig. 29). Then the right flap across the left, bending the cap into a hat shape.

Staple it in place. (fig. 30). Next, just bend (and crease) the lower front corners of the hat upward to form the "wings." Secure the cap with white shoestrings tied to the sides. Too cute!

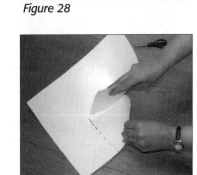
Figure 28

Figure 29

The collar is simple to make, too. Just enlarge and cut out the pattern on page 39 (fig. 30). Cut the center and front out as shown. Then simply place the collar around the child's head and connect the cut ends with a brad. Easy! And it looks great over a black shirt!

Figure 30

Native American Feather Headbands

You'll need:

- Colorful construction paper, or
- Poster board and paint
- Tape

- Scissors
- Tall feathers (optional)

Figure 31

Cut a two-inch wide headband to fit around the child's forehead. Color it with fun patterns and tape it in place. Cut a tall feather out of construction paper or poster board, or use a real feather and tape it to the *back* of the headband (fig. 31).

Star Costume (Fig. 32)

You'll need:

- Poster board (white)
- Spray glitter (gold)
- Gold lamé fabric, 2 yards (optional)
- Fray-Check™ (or zig-zag the edges)
- Scissors
- Hot glue
- Star pattern (see fig. 20, page 32 and use an opaque projector to enlarge it to fit a piece of poster board)

Make a T-robe from the gold lamé, as shown for the Bible tunic on page 25. Cut it to mid-calf. Then cut zig-zags to the knee (about 8 inches long and 6 inches wide). These don't have to be perfect in any way. Machine baste the edges or use a product

like Fray-Check™ to keep the edges from fraying. For best results, apply this carefully with a small paintbrush while the garment is hanging.

While the Fray-Check™ dries, enlarge and cut out your star pattern. In the very center, cut out a hole for the child's face. Don't cut it too large! It should fit comfortably over the child's face. Use a hair pin or clip to secure the star to the hair.

Spray the front of the star with gold paint, then with glitter paint. Let it dry; then spray the back in the same way.

The child will wear the gold tunic with the giant star over his or her face. Absolutely stellar!

Figure 32

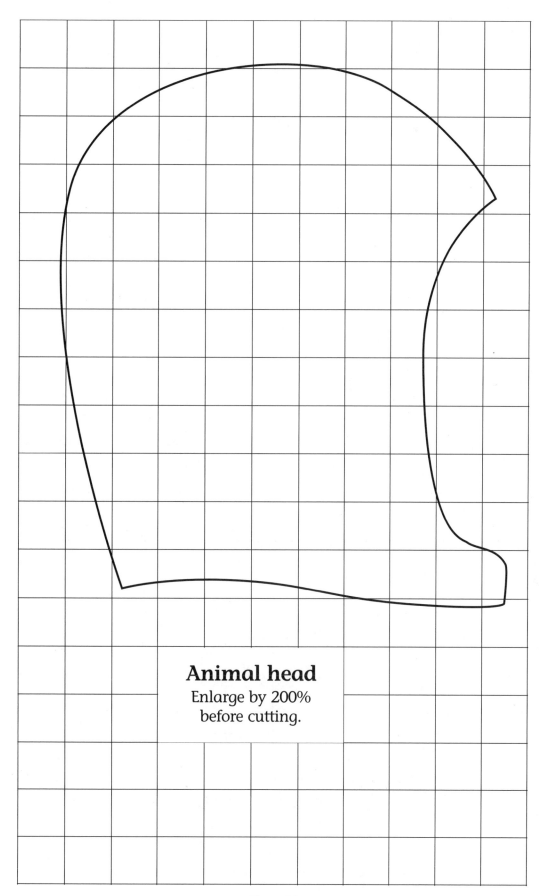

Animal head
Enlarge by 200%
before cutting.

Figure 15

**Animal center
headpiece.**
Enlarge by 200%
before cutting.

Pilgrim Collar Pattern
Enlarge by 200%

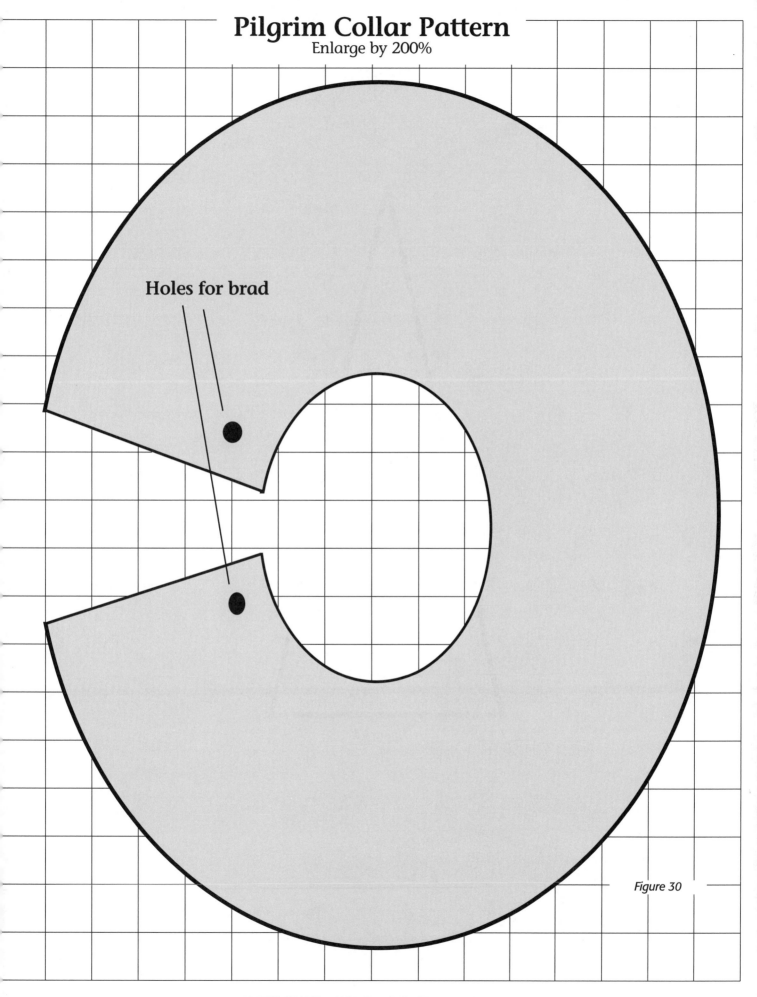

Holes for brad

Figure 30

CROWN PATTERN

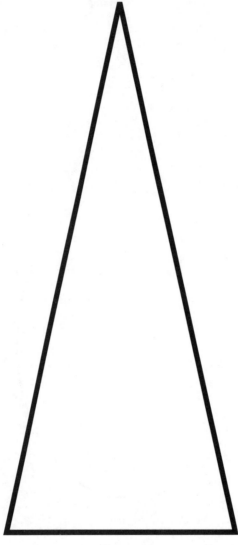

Figure 24

StaGinG, ARRanGinG anD BLoCKinG

You have a choir of 30 kids and they're all wearing top hats! How can you arrange them so that all of their faces show?

This chapter is about positioning and blocking. *Blocking* is the theatrical term that describes placing kids on the stage and moving them from scene to scene. Keep in mind some simple but important points that will help you arrange your choir and cast so they can all be seen and heard.

CHoiR

If your church has risers or a choir loft, you're better off than most. Risers enable you to arrange children in tiers so they can be seen. And this is important, because

Never use rows of chairs for risers, even for rehearsals! Folding chairs can collapse and non-folding chairs can and do tip over.

there will be parents out there taking photos and videos who want to get adorable shots of their kids.

Risers are risky for preschoolers. By all means keep them off the back row. Whenever you can place risers against a wall, you avoid potential falls and injuries. Emphasize that risers are not an acceptable place to run, jump and play. That's for outside!

Arrange kids on risers with the tallest children on the back row. Each row should reach its highest point in the center with the shortest children on the ends. If it is important to you to have strong singers in the front row, and they happen to be tall, arrange them on the ends of the rows. Generally, though, a good strong voice somewhere in the back or middle will encourage those in front to sing out!

Soloists should come out of their rows before their songs begin and stand to the side until it's their turn to sing. The director should cue them to walk forward to the microphone in time to sing their parts. After the solo, the child should step back and join the chorus.

CHOIRS WITH NO RISERS

Not every church has a choir loft, neither can every church afford to buy or rent risers. So what can these folks do with many children of varying heights? Here are a few suggestions:

1. Build portable platforms in six-inch and 12-inch heights. Volunteers handy with a hammer and saw can build these easily. Platforms should be about two feet in depth and about four feet wide for easy portability and stacking.

2. If platforms are out of the question, try arranging your kids in two rows with the tallest kids in back, shortest in front, in "checkerboard" rows. This means kids are two feet apart in the back row. In the front row, kids stand in front of the gaps formed by the back row. It's not a perfect solution, but will allow more little faces to shine through!

3. This option will work better for the less formal songs and productions: Have back row kids stand; middle row kids sit in chairs, and front row kids sit on the floor. For some churches this will not be a good option because most people in the congregation will not see kids seated on the floor. Again, work with what you have for the best possible outcome.

BLOCKING

One very important stage rule that will guide you as you block is that the speaker should never give the audience his or her back. This means that a child delivering a line to another child should take great pains not to turn so far sideways that he or she is actually positioned more toward the wall. Here are some very basic tips that can help keep this from happening:

When talking to someone on stage left or right, face the person, keeping the shoulder that is closest to the audience slightly behind the other. This turns your chest toward the audience (fig. 34).

Never show the

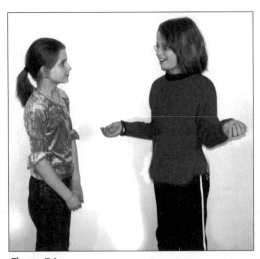

Figure 34

audience your back while you're speaking. Figure 35 illustrates this incorrect stance.

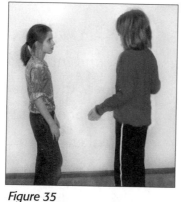

Figure 35

Figure 36

Keep the leg closest to the audience slightly behind you. This, too, will help turn your front, without completely facing the audience (fig. 36).

Avoid using the hand closest to the

Figure 37

Figure 38

audience in any way that will block your body. For example, if you have to place a hand on someone's shoulder, use the arm furthest from the crowd (see fig. 37). Figure 38 illustrates the wrong way to do this. Notice how the arm in this illustration causes both characters to be obscured. If an actor needs to pick up a glass of water, have him use the arm furthest from the front of the stage. This keeps him "open" and unobstructed.

Other things to remember:

"Crossing" another character— that is, deliberately walking in front of him—is a symbol of

power. When a character crosses others, it demeans the others, giving the impression that he has the upper hand in a situation. (fig. 39).

If trying to elevate a character to having power over another character in a conversation, put the stronger character in a position that's physically "above" the other. For example, have the scolded person be sitting. Even if he's taller than the scolder, he appears to be shrinking emotionally (fig. 40).

Figure 39

Figure 40

Mikes, Tykes and EQ

Speech on stage is best understood with microphones. Well, okay, sometimes. It's not very easy to understand someone when the squeal of feedback is whistling through your speakers! It's annoying to say the least. And kids are great at making it happen!

How can you avoid feedback? First of all, the kids need to know the proper way to use a mike—no yelling into it, no pressing their lips against it and making "hoo" sounds (why does every child do this?). Avoiding these things is a matter of training and discipline by the director. But some feedback can be avoided technically. Of course, it's best avoided by having a really dependable tech person running the sound. But if your sound guy or gal is a novice, here are a few cues:

- Practice volume levels during rehearsal and try to keep them there. (You might allow for a one-point increase in volume if the crowd is fairly thick. Sound will not be the same in a full sanctuary.)

- Never have a monitor facing the microphone or you will get feedback. This is when the sound (voices, whispers, every sound in the building!) goes through the system, is amplified, and is directed into the microphone again, only to be sent through the system with more amplification! This "sound multiplication" causes the squeal that raises neck hair. Keep the microphone out of the direction of the speakers and monitors. Remember, the speaker sounds "fan out."

- You might have an equalizer built into your system. This gizmo enables you to compensate for the highs and lows built into certain sounds (voices, music, etc.). Set the levels so that the treble is not too high (too much treble, or "highs," makes the voice sound tinny and thin and ultimately creates a hiss). Likewise, make sure that the bass is not set too high (too much bass, or "lows," makes things sound muffled and boomy). If you have a simple bass and treble knob on your system, start with them both set to the middle. For kids who tend to mumble in the mike, you may have to raise the treble a bit and lower the bass. While too much treble can sound gratingly tinny, a little bit, tastefully used, can make words more crisp and understandable.

If you have EQ sliders on your system (a bunch of sliding knobs in a row), try positioning them into a slight smile or "U" shape! This sounds silly, but lots of sound-folk try that setting first.

And now a word about lapel mikes.

They're the clip-on kind that lots of pastors are using today instead of the hand-held or stand-up variety. The microphone clips to your lapel. A little wire attached to the mike leads to a little beeper-sized box that hooks to the back of a belt or slips into a pocket. Lapel mikes allow for ease of movement so your actors don't have to look stiff and unnatural standing in front of a microphone. There are a couple of things to remember when using lapel mikes:

Install a fresh battery before the program. A low battery can cause the mike signal to come in and out, which is very annoying, and prevents the audience from hearing what your little actors have to say.

Find the right place to clip the mike during a rehearsal. Clipping it under a loose, draped costume can cause rustling sounds from the fabric rubbing on the microphone. There can be terrible distorting sounds with every move the child makes. Just make sure it's free from the folds and drapes of a costume so the child's voice will be the only noise amplified.

This point is *so* important! Always make sure the technician turns the mike all the way up before the child's turn to speak, and all the way down when the skit is over!

Let me share one of my stage production bloopers that had to do with a lapel mike. One of the actors finished his part, then exited to the basement. But on the way he stopped off at the bathroom where he did what he stopped to do, then flushed the toilet like a good boy. And yes, the entire audience of 1,000 heard the whole thing from trickle to ka-whoosh! Hence the lesson: keep tabs on whose mikes should be up or down!

CONTROLLING THE WIGGLE WORMS

Almost every kids' program I've ever seen has unknowingly starred a front-row scratcher, a kid who can't keep his fingers away from his nose, or a little girl who pulls her dress over her head. I've seen them all, including a little four-year-old who literally pulled her arms out of the sleeves of her dress while looking up at the bright lights above her. She couldn't see anybody in the audience, and never seemed to wonder why the entire congregation was howling with laughter!

Inappropriate onstage behavior is very difficult to prevent in young children, but some can be avoided by reminding the children that they should always be watching you, the director. If you have their attention, you can keep them doing what they should be doing and the rest won't even be an issue. As you rehearse in your classroom, teach proper behavior. If your kids are picking their noses in class, they'll likely do it onstage and the moment will be forever imprinted in someone's videocam. So, you can either teach these dos and don'ts:

- Don't pick your nose.
- Don't pull up your shirt or your dress.
- Don't play with your clothing in any way.
- Don't scratch inappropriately.
- Do keep your hands at your sides.
- Do try not to yawn.
- Don't talk to your neighbor during the performance.

Or you can make it a lot more positive by turning it into one simple rule:

- Always keep your eyes on me.

If kids follow that rule, they'll avoid embarrassing and distracting behaviors.

Encourage kids not to wave to parents and friends in the audience until they're taking their final bows. While a little childlike behavior may make your program endearing, careful stage etiquette keeps the message from being upstaged by the distracting things kids might be tempted to do when they're performing.

Stage Management

You can smoothly organize your larger productions with just a little knowledge about stage management.

Dressing Rooms

First of all, establish dressing areas. You'll need two—one for boys and one for girls. It's best not to use the restrooms that the rest of the congregation will use. It can be uncomfortable for a guest to enter a restroom filled with giggly, half-dressed children, clothing and costumes strewn all over the floor and the sink blockaded with little girls putting on lipstick. Arrange for another room.

The Green Room

In the world of theater and television, a room called a "Green Room" is the place where actors wait to be called to the stage. Your Green Room doesn't have to be green, but for fun you could tape a green piece of construction paper on the door, or even decorate the room with green crepe paper so kids will know it's the Green Room.

Security

Unfortunately, a church building cannot be considered the safest place on earth. Strangers are—and should be—free to enter, but children should be taught that the same rules of safety apply whether in the mall or in the church.

Never let a child go to the restroom alone when a show is underway. It's a good idea to have responsible helpers on the night or day of the program who can escort children, in groups of two or more, for restroom breaks.

Keep children in designated areas—don't let them wander the halls or peek into the sanctuary during the program. They should be kept occupied in the supervised Green Room until called, both for security reasons and for noise control.

Backstage Entertainment

One of the greatest things we ever did for our church Green Room was to install a television where children could watch the program transmitted through a video camera. With the use of long cables, we wired a video camera to the downstairs TV. The cast was able to watch the program as it was being performed. This helped keep kids occupied and ready for their scenes at the same time.

If you can't hook up a video cam, you might want to put a TV in the Green Room anyway and show Christian video cartoons such as those in the Godprints™ series or Veggie Tales™. It will be much easier to control a large group of children if you offer this kind of pastime.

While kids are bound to squirm and wiggle, make it clear that when it's "show time" they need to refrain from playing physical games that could compromise costumes and make up. If television isn't an option, have helpers set out board games and books.

Making those Entrances

If you have a rather large or complex production, you'll need several people to help keep entrances and exits happening at the right time. Ideally, all stage management and technical personnel will wear headsets that allow them to communicate with the stage manager or director through a single channel. This is great when the cast must wait in a Green Room that's far from the stage. You may be able to rent headsets for a couple of nights if purchasing them is out of the question.

If obtaining headsets isn't possible, mark the script for a summoning place well in advance of each child's entrance. At that part in the script, a runner should bring the child from the Green Room to the stage entrance, then stand by to listen for the entrance cue. You'll want to be sure to give your actors plenty of time to catch their breath before they go on!

Christmas Pageants

*T*he annual Christmas pageant is always a memorable night for kids and parents alike. If you were raised in the church, you probably have vivid memories of dressing up like an angel with a glittering halo, or being a shepherd in a bathrobe with a rope belt and thinking how funny it was to wear a bathrobe to church!

Christmas pageants can be as elaborate as you choose. Some churches have brought in camels, donkeys and flying angels on wires for spectacle! When you're putting on a program solely by kids, things can be MUCH simpler and still be inspiring and fun.

You'll find two Christmas programs in this section. The first is a quick and easy traditional program with most of the speaking done by a narrator. The second is an intermediate program with a modern twist. It involves several characters with speaking parts and some original music.

One Silent Night

(quick and easy)

If you have lots of kids you want to use in this program, keep in mind that you can have a whole host of angels—boys and girls. Remind the boys (who sometimes see angels as sissies) that the messenger angel who identified himself was Gabriel, not Gabrielle! However, if you only have girls, Gabrielle might be what you need!

You may also "herd" lots of little ones into becoming a flock of sheep. The outfits are easy and the result is adorable! The rest of the cast can wear whatever Bibletime costumes you have available.

Cast: Narrator, Child 1, Child 2, Child 3, Child 4, Shepherds, Sheep, Angels, Mary, Joseph, Wise Men

Props: Doll for baby Jesus, manger, gifts for the wise men to carry

Set: Use a simple backdrop of the area near Bethlehem. Show an outline of Bethlehem with a city wall on the left, running off the backdrop. To the right, indicate rural countryside, including a hillside where shepherds and sheep will gather. (See page 109 for a sample backdrop.) If you wish, add potted fig trees or succulent plants here and there. Dim the lighting, then add a spot for starlight and some soft lighting in the town for an evening scene.

Arranging the Choir: Arrange the choir in three groups: two to enter from the sides of the stage, and one to enter from the back of the auditorium. Have the children with speaking or acting parts wait offstage in order of their appearance. Keep them out of sight so their pre-entrance fidgets don't become an unplanned side show! If there's no hallway where they can wait, put up a room divider or screen. Be sure to have an adult helper right there to keep things calm and help them make their entrances at the right time.

If you're working with a small group of children and need all of them in the choir, have those with individual parts stand at the sides so they can move to act out their parts, then rejoin the choir.

THE Pageant

NARRATOR: Welcome! Thank you for joining us to celebrate the birth of our Savior. We invite you to pause from the hustle and bustle of the season and travel back in time to a small village in the countryside of Judah. The village isn't quite as peaceful as usual because it's tax time! The great emperor, Caesar Augustus, has ordered everyone to go to their home towns to be counted. So everyone from the family of David has crowded into Bethlehem.

Have the children who will form the choir enter from the front and both sides of the stage, jostling each other a bit and complaining.

CHILD 1: Oh, my aching feet!

CHILD 2: Do you think we'll be able to get a room tonight?

CHILD 3: I'm hungry!

CHILD 4: *(Loudly.)* Are we there yet?

The children assemble on the left side of the stage to form the choir.

NARRATOR: The streets of the little town are bursting! People are cranky and dusty and tired of being jostled by the crowds. Paying taxes is no fun at all, especially when all the money goes to the big, bossy Romans who think they rule the world. (Actually, they do!) But night is falling at last, and as the sun dips below the horizon, peace settles over the village.

Dim the lights.

Soft starlight shines from the sky. Here and there lamplight glows from a window.

Add soft lighting.

And as weary travelers and townfolk settle in for the night, they have no idea that everything is about to change....

SONG: O, LITTLE TOWN OF BETHLEHEM

LUKE 2:9

NARRATOR: On a hillside not too far from town, shepherds gather their flocks into a little group where they will be snug and warm.

Shepherds and sheep enter and assemble on the right side of the stage. The sheep baa softly, snuggle up together and go to sleep. One sheep tries to sneak off, but a shepherd directs him back to the group, shaking his finger. The sheep baas his objection, then settles down to sleep with the others. One shepherd goes to the mike.

LUKE 2: 8,9

SHEPHERD 1: And there were shepherds living out in the fields nearby, keeping watch over their flocks at night. An angel of the Lord appeared to them, and the glory of the Lord shone around them, and they were terrified.

Shepherd 1 runs to rejoin his companions. All the shepherds and sheep quake in fear. The sheep hang onto each other for security. Angel 1 enters and goes to the mike.

LUKE 2:10

ANGEL 1: Do not be afraid. I bring you good news of great joy that will be for all the people. Today in the town of David a Savior has been born to you; he is Christ the Lord.

All angels enter.

NARRATOR: Suddenly a great company of the heavenly host appeared with the angel, praising God and saying,

LUKE 2:14

ALL ANGELS: Glory to God in the highest, and on earth peace to men on whom his favor rests.

Angels join the choir.

SONG: ANGELS WE HAVE HEARD ON HIGH

As the choir sings, Mary and Joseph enter carrying Baby Jesus. They lay Jesus in manger at center stage. The shepherds leave the flock and join the scene at the manger. The wayward sheep wants to follow, but a shepherd shakes his finger at the sheep again. The sheep goes back and lies down with the others.

LUKE : 2:15,16

NARRATOR: So the shepherds hurried off and found Mary and Joseph, and the baby, who was lying in the manger.

✓SONG: AWAY IN A MANGER

LUKE 2:17

NARRATOR: When they had seen him, they spread the word concerning what had been told them about this child. The shepherds returned, glorifying and praising God for all the things they had heard and seen, which were just as they had been told.

✓SONG: GO TELL IT ON THE MOUNTAIN

During the song, the shepherds join the choir.

MATTHEW 2: 1,2

NARRATOR: After Jesus was born in Bethlehem in Judea, during the time of King Herod, Magi from the east came to Jerusalem and asked, "Where is the one who has been born king of the Jews? We saw his star in the east and have come to worship him."

Piano plays first line of "We Three Kings" as the wise men enter in a slow, dignified manner, carrying gifts. They process toward the manger.

MATTHEW 2: 9, 10

NARRATOR: After they had heard the king, they went on their way, and the star they had seen in the east went ahead of them until it stopped over the place where the child was. When they saw the star, they were overjoyed.

The Wise Men lay their gifts by the manger, then kneel.

NARRATOR: Please join us in singing.

✓SONG: O COME ALL YE FAITHFUL

During this song, the sheep and the children in the choir assemble around the manger. The sheep curl up on the floor, the wise men and shepherds kneel, the angels and the rest of the choir stand.

NARRATOR: God sent his Son into the world that peaceful, starlit night. While the village of Bethlehem slept, hope was born. Only a few people were aware of what God was doing in the world. Now we join the shepherds and the wise men and God's people throughout the ages who worshiped the tiny Savior King, the light of the world.

✓SONG: SILENT NIGHT

Have the children leave the stage and fill the aisles as they sing, until only Joseph and Mary are on stage with Baby Jesus.

NARRATOR: We are here because we know that this baby is Christ the Lord. The hope he brings shines through darkness. The forgiveness he offers is free to anyone who believes. And the life he gives never ends! May the wonder of that silent night live in your heart. Live in the light of his love; go in his peace.

The End

The Christmas Star

(intermediate)

Cast: Show Host (child or adult), Star, Mary, Joseph, Wise Men, Shepherds, Soldiers, Angel(s), Herod, Sheep, Santa Claus (may be an adult). The Show Host can wear a glittery tux; or a white shirt (open collar), black vest and trousers, and a top hat and cane would be great. The showier the better. If a Santa suit is beyond your means, trim red sweats with white fur. Add black boots, a wide belt over a pillow-padded tummy, and a fur-trimmed Santa hat.

Props: Doll for baby Jesus, manger (a cardboard box filled with straw will do), mallet for Joseph; unfinished stool or birdhouse for Joseph; staffs for shepherds.

Dressing tables, powder puffs, brushes, etc., are a plus for the set.

Set: The stage should be as uncluttered as possible. Remove all furniture and set up a plain backdrop. String Christmas lights around the backdrop and the front of the stage. Broadway-type floor lights are a luxury, but if you have access to them, use them!

For a jazzier set, place stools and dressing tables at each side of the stage. The "contestants" can sit at the tables and primp while they're waiting to be next. It's important that they remain silent and keep from drawing too much attention to themselves.

● ●

THE PAGEANT

The entire cast appears for the opening song. Have them file in and find their positions as a choir, then sing. Remember, this is sort of a mock-Broadway revue, so encourage the kids to be animated, smile and bounce to the music.

CHOIR: A SHOW TONIGHT
(Music on page 56–57.)

There's a show tonight!
It's December twenty-four.
We've got lots of lights,
Red and green and so much more.
And don't forget our special guest.
We won't say who, no,

You have to guess.
So don't you move,
Just stay right where you are.
You're gonna meet the Christmas star!

Have the pianist or other musicians continue to play the song softly while the kids with acting/speaking parts scurry offstage. Host takes off his hat for a moment and tucks his cane under his arm as he speaks.

HOST: That's right, folks, the star of Christmas is right here! And who is it? Well, we'll let you decide! (*Points the cane toward the audience on the word "you," and moves* *backward and to the right while the first contestant enters.)*

Star of Bethlehem enters and sings the song below, preening and acting like a prima donna.

SOLO: STAR SONG
(Music on page 58.)

I'm the greatest star!
I'm so shiny and bright
Ev'rybody was watching me
That first Christmas night!

HOST: True, there was a star in the East that lit the sky over Bethlehem.

STAR: Not just any star! ME!

HOST: Whoever. But, sorry. You're not the greatest star.

The star gives a pouty look and walks off in a huff.

HOST: Next we have Mary, a young mother with a very special baby!

Mary enters cradling her baby. She takes the baby to the manger and lays him down there while the kids are singing Mary's Little Lamb. Then she returns to the center of the stage and remains meek and humble.

CHOIR: MARY'S LITTLE LAMB
(Music on page 59.)

[Tune of *Mary Had a Little Lamb*]
Mary had a little lamb,
Little lamb, little lamb.
Mary had a little lamb,
The Lamb of God called Jesus!
(repeat)

HOST: A big hand for Mary!

[APPLAUSE]

CHILD 1: So is Mary the Christmas Star?

HOST: No…it's not Mary.

Mary smiles and bows slightly, then exits.

HOST: Next we have Joseph, the carpenter. He was a very kind man. He took care of Mary and her newborn son.

Joseph enters with a mallet and an unfinished wooden stool or birdhouse. He sings the song below.

SOLO: JOSEPH'S SONG
(Music on page 60.)

[Tune of *Itsy Bitsy Spider*]
My name is Joseph,
A carpenter by trade.
I married Mary,
By her side I stayed.
I took care of Jesus
And it sure made me glad
To raise the son of God
As his adoptive dad!

APPLAUSE. Joseph bows humbly.

CHILD 1: So is Joseph the star of Christmas?

Joseph shakes his head "NO."

HOST: No. He is not the star either!

Joseph exits as the Wise Men enter.

CHILD 2 and CHILD 3: WOW! These guys must be stars!

CHILD 1: Without a doubt!

Choir and Wise Men sing

SONG: WE THREE KINGS

CHILD 2: So, which one is the star?

HOST: Nice clothes, but not star material. They came to give gifts to the newborn king and…

From the left, Herod jumps onstage energetically.

HEROD: *(To the audience.)* King? Did I hear someone say *king?* There's no king but ME around here! Understand? King Herod! And don't you forget it!

HOST: Excuse me, sir, but this is a star search, not the Gong Show!

HEROD: Star search, eh? All the more reason for me to be here! And what's this talk about a newborn king? Do I look like I was born yesterday?

HOST: You're not the one—

HEROD: Then I'd better do something and do it fast! Soldiers! Come!

Soldiers march in and salute together.

SOLDIERS: Sir!

HEROD: Some wise guys tell me there's a newborn king out there. That means he's going to grow up and take over what's mine! Well I won't have it! So go out there and get rid of him! Understand?

SOLDIERS: Sir! Yes, Sir!

Soldiers march out.

HEROD: *(With an evil look.)* It's all under control! Ha-ha-ha-ha-ha-ha!

HOST: Sorry. I've read the story and you lose.

HEROD: Waahhh!

Herod exits.

CHILD 4: So if Herod wasn't the star of Christmas, what about the shepherds and the angels? They had a big part on the first Christmas night.

Shepherds enter. One lies on the ground, propped up on one elbow, picking at the ground. Another twirls his staff. A third sits on a rock, yawning.

SHEPHERD 1: Silent night, boring night.

SHEPHERD 2: Yeah. Except for that big star in the sky.

SHEPHERD 3: So it's big. Big and boring. Stars are a dime a dozen. I hate third shift.

Suddenly Gabriel jumps out onstage, followed by other angels. The shepherds shriek and fall down.

ANGEL GABRIEL: Fear not!

SHEPHERD 1: Easy for you to say!

ANGEL GABRIEL: I bring good news. A Savior's been born—Christ the Lord! You'll find him wrapped in cloths and lying in a manger.

SHEPHERD 2: Wow!

SHEPHERD 4: Yeah, wow!

SHEPHERD 3: Guess it's not such a boring night after all!

CHOIR: ANGELS WE HAVE HEARD ON HIGH

Shepherds and angels exit.

CHILD 1: So was the star of Christmas a shepherd or an angel?

HOST: Neither! Now you've seen a lot of famous people. But not one of them is the real star of Christmas. The real star of Christmas is…

CHILD 2: I know! Santa Claus!

CHILD 3: Must be! Just look at the stores! Santa Clauses are everywhere! He must be the star!

HOST: That's what lots of kids, young and old, often think. See, long ago a man named Nicholas gave gifts to poor children at Christmas. Over the years, people have gradually given Saint Nick the higher place of honor. But I don't think he would have liked that very much, because all of his gift-giving was inspired by the <u>real</u> star of Christmas.

Santa enters shaking his head and sings the song below

SOLO: SANTA'S SONG
(Music on page 61–62.)

Ev'rywhere you look you see
A Santa Claus.
My image reigns
As if I were the Christmas cause.
Children think of me all night, for toys
I'll bring by morning's light.
But I am not the star,
I am not the star,
I am not the Christmas Star.
I am not the star, I am not the star,

I am not the Christmas Star.

HOST: That's right. There's someone much more important. And the gift he gave us is greater than any other gift we could ever receive! It's the gift of forgiveness of sins. It's a gift that brings eternal life! Because of the star, we can live forever!

The entire cast enters and sings.

CHOIR: JESUS IS THE STAR
(Music on page 63–64.)

The star of Christmas
Is really rather small,
Isn't flashy, doesn't really stand out at all.
He came to earth as humbly as could be,
And he came to save the world
That means you and me.
He was just a baby when he came to earth.
There was nothing glamorous about his birth!

Mary and Joseph enter and kneel by the manger as the song continues.

Jesus is the star!
Jesus is the star!
Jesus is the Christmas star!

HOST: So there you have it folks! Jesus is the Christmas star! Not Santa, not Rudolph, not even Shepherds or Wise Men! It's Jesus! And he didn't stay a baby. He grew up and gave his life for us. Even more, he rose again. That means we can live forever too! And that's exactly why we sing, "Joy to the World! " Stand with us and sing!

CHOIR AND CONGREGATION: JOY TO THE WORLD

The End

A Show Tonight

Words and Music by
Susan D. Parsons

There's a

show to-night! It's De- cem- ber twen- ty four.

We've got Christ-mas lights red and green and so much

more.   And don't for- get   our   spe- cial guest.   We

won't say who,   no,   you   have to guess.   So   don't you   move,   just stay

right where you are! You're gon- na'   meet   the Christ- mas   Star!

Star Song

Words & Music by
Susan D. Parsons

I'm the grea- test star! I'm so shi- ny and bright Ev- 'ry bo- dy was watch- in' me that first Christ- mas night. night!

Mary's Little Lamb

Traditional
Melody

Words by
Susan D. Parsons

Joseph's Song

Words by
Susan D. Parsons

Tune of Itsy Bitsy Spider

Santa's Song

Words and Music by
Susan D. Parsons

Jesus Is the Star

Words and Music by
Susan D. Parsons

save the world that means you and me. He was just a

ba- by when He came to earth. There was no- thing gla- mor- ous a-

bout His birth! Oh JE-SUS is the star! JE-SUS is the

star! JE- SUS is the Christ- mas Star!

Easter Pageants

*T*he Easter story straight from God's Word is so full of the miraculous that it's hard for us to take in. This is when a pageant can be one of your most effective ministry tools. Even a simple pageant helps both participants and observers move along the path from intellectual acceptance to joyful understanding. Watching characters travel the emotional gamut from despair to joy, even if they are portrayed by child actors and singers, lends a new layer of meaning to the mystery of Jesus' journey from death to life that never ends.

How do you deal with the distraction of bunnies and baskets? Little Easter feasters sometimes come to church more excited about stuffed animals, treats and fancy new clothes than about the resurrection. And who can blame them? The secular trappings of Easter are concrete and immediately gratifying. The story of Jesus is much harder to grasp. A fair number of kids haven't dealt with death at all, so Jesus' stunning victory doesn't touch them at an experiential level.

But drama does! Participating in an Easter pageant pulls ancient truth off the written page and right into their lives. Whether you choose the traditional "What Happened in the Garden" or the contemporary "Nobunny Knows," you'll provide a wonderful opportunity for members of your congregation, young and old, to embrace the glory of Easter.

What Happened in the Garden

(intermediate)

Cast: Narrator, Bud, Bloomer, Mary 1, Mary 2, Salome, Angel, Choir

The Narrator can be a child or adult. Dress Mary 1, Mary 2 and Salome in simple Bibletime costumes. Bud and Bloomer are flowers. Dress them in green sweats or leotards. Add fabric or posterboard "petals" around their necks. The Angel can wear a simple white robe.

Scene: Create a path across the stage area with construction paper stepping stones. Or simply have two kids outline the path with crepe paper streamers as the performance begins. A cardboard tomb with a large rolling stone is great, but the play works without it. For a more elaborate presentation, see page 110 for backdrop ideas.

THE PAGEANT

The choir files in and stands at the left side of the stage. BUD and BLOOMER enter and crouch beside the path with their heads down.

NARRATOR: It's Sunday morning in a Jerusalem garden. The year is 32 AD. The sun has just risen, and all is quiet. But if you listen very carefully, you might be able to hear a conversation between two flowers on the path.

Bud and Bloomer rise, stretch and yawn.

BUD: I don't even feel like blooming.

BLOOMER: Why? What's the matter, Bud?

BUD: Everything just seems wrong since Jesus died. I mean, he was there at the very creation of the world, Bloomer. Now he's dead. Maybe we should just wilt and give up.

BLOOMER: I know what you mean. Why did those guys kill him? He healed people. He fed people. He showed us what God is like. He gave life. And then they took life away from him on a horrible, awful cross. It doesn't make sense.

BUD: Do you remember that earthquake when he died?

BLOOMER: You bet I do. My roots were rockin'. I even lost a few petals.

BUD: And when those Roman soldiers rolled that stone in front of his tomb, they missed me by inches. I was this far from bein' potpourri.

BLOOMER: Potpour-*who?*

BUD: Never mind.

Booming sound effects to indicate an earthquake. Flowers start to shake.

BLOOMER: Whoa-ho-ho! It's happening again?

BUD: Hey, look—the stone is moving. Hit the dirt!

Flowers duck and cover their heads. The Angel enters and moves the stone from the front of the tomb, or makes a push motion to indicate that's what's happening. Angel stands "at ease" and freezes. Flowers stand up cautiously.

BLOOMER: The stone moved! Jesus' tomb is open!

BUD: (*Dusting himself off.*) Fortunately it rolled in the other direction this time. *Pauses and raises hands to ears.* Listen! I hear people coming. Mum's the word.

BLOOMER: (*Indignantly.*) I'm not a mum— I'm a daisy.

Bud and Bloomer freeze as Mary, Salome and the other Mary come down the path, then pause center stage.

NARRATOR: Three friends came to the tomb to prepare Jesus' body with special spices and perfumes. But they didn't know what had happened in the garden.

MARY 1: These spices should have been placed with Jesus' body as soon as he was put there! That's the Jewish tradition!

MARY 2: But there wasn't enough time. The sun had already set, so it was the Sabbath. And you can't anoint the dead on the Sabbath! That's the Jewish tradition!

SALOME: The best we can do is anoint Jesus' body *today.* Now the problem is going to be that big stone that Pilate put over the door. How can we move such a big stone?

MARY 1: Stone? What stone? Look! It's been rolled away!

The women peer toward the tomb and look astonished—hands to cheeks, hand covering mouth, rubbing eyes and looking again. Mary 1 rushes toward the tomb.

MARY 2: Jesus is gone! (*She looks at the Angel.*) Where have you taken him?

SALOME: Oh, no! This is terrible! Someone stole the body of our Lord!

ANGEL: Why are you looking for a living person in a place for the dead? He's not here. He is risen from the dead. Remember, he told you he would be crucified by sinful men, then buried, and then he would rise again?

SALOME: Yes! He did say that! How did you know?

ANGEL: Go and tell Peter and John and the others. Your Lord lives!

The flowers jump up and down and clap.

BUD AND BLOOMER: Woohoo! Yippee!

The girls turn around to look at them, but they freeze again.

CHOIR SONG: THE EASTER SONG

by Steve Green

©The Sparrow Corporation

(Available in many worship books at your local Christian bookstore. Use your web search engine to find legal downloads of the lyrics. CDs available from 2ndchapterofacts.com.)

MARY 2: It's a miracle!

SALOME: Jesus is risen, just as he said!

MARY 1: We should hurry and tell the others.

The girls rush off. Bud and Bloomer jump and cheer again.

BUD: Jesus died, then rose again.

BLOOMER: I don't get it. How could that happen?

BUD: By God's power! Do you remember what it was like to be a bulb, all dark and cold inside the earth?

BLOOMER: Sure. Then the warm sunlight poured down on us and we pushed through the earth. Oh—I get it!

BUD: Jesus died and was buried—just like we were when we were little bulbs. But he was stronger than death. He won! And that's the bloomin' truth!

Bud, Bloomer, Mary 1, Mary 2 and Salome join the choir.

NARRATOR: And because he lives, you can live. Today we celebrate the death of death and the gift of life Jesus offers through his resurrection from the dead. Join us in singing, "He Lives!"

CHOIR AND CONGREGATION SONG: HE LIVES (I Serve a Risen Savior)

All the children exit after the last verse.

The End

Nobunny Knows

(intermediate)

Cast: Ryan, Jenna, Mike, Paige, Choir

You'll need a bunny costume, a lamb costume and an Easter basket costume (a box painted baby blue with basket weave design and handle, and worn around the waist by Mike—glue some Easter grass around the top and let Mike wear pastel sweat pants and shirt.

Scene: Typical neighborhood. See page 111 for backdrop ideas.

● ●

THE PAGEANT

SCENE 1: *The kids' choir waits offstage. Ryan enters from the left and crosses the stage, carrying his backpack home from school. At center stage, he sees his shoe is untied. He puts his backpack down and bends down to tie his shoe. Then Jenna and Mike enter from behind and see him.*

JENNA: Hey, Ryan! Are you going to the Easter party at John's house?

RYAN: Probably.

He tightens his other shoelace.

JENNA: You're supposed to wear an Easter costume, you know. I'm going as an Easter bunny, since that's what Easter is mostly about. Paige has a lamb costume. That's kind of Easter-y too. What are you going to be?

RYAN: I don't know. I never even thought about it.

MIKE: He's going as an egg! Ha! All he has to do is paint his head!

Ryan smiles and shakes his head at Mike's remark.

JENNA: Whoa—that's not too nice, Mike. Especially considering what your own costume is.

Ryan stands up and starts putting on his backpack.

RYAN: What's your costume, Mike?

MIKE: I'm going as an Easter basket!

JENNA: How lame is that?

MIKE: It's not lame—I wear this cardboard box painted blue with a handle that goes over my head and Easter grass sticking out all over. Pretty cool.

JENNA: Whatever. Marcy's going as a marshmallow chick. Her mom made this cool costume out of mattress foam painted yellow! So what are you going to be?

RYAN: I told you, I haven't thought about it yet.

JENNA: Well, you'd better start thinking about it. The party is Saturday. There's a prize for the best costume. We're gonna hunt for eggs and everything! I love Easter! Don't you?

RYAN: (Seriously and thoughtfully.) Yeah—Easter is the best.

MIKE: What's your favorite part? Mine's the Easter basket, of course. Especially the chocolate bunny I get every year. But I don't like hollow bunnies. Solid milk chocolate's the best.

JENNA: My favorite part is coloring eggs! I make up my own colors by mixing them. So, Ryan. What's your favorite part? Bunnies?

RYAN: (Without any sarcasm or "attitude.") No.

MIKE: Malted milk robin's eggs?

RYAN: No.

JENNA: It's a mystery! **No bunny knows!** Get it? No **bunny** knows?! Come on Mike. We've got to get home. See you later, Ryan. Mystery man!

Jenna and Mike exit. Ryan stays behind for a moment and shuffles, kicking the ground.

RYAN: (Sighing.) She doesn't know how true that is. No **bunny** could ever know. That's because Easter doesn't have much to do with bunnies or candy at all.

SONG: NO BUNNY KNOWS
(Music on page 72–74)

No bunny knows
What Easter means to me,
'Cause Easter means that Jesus

Died upon a tree.
And after Jesus died
Up from the grave he rose.
That's a mystery
That no bunny knows.

No bunny knows
That I can live again,
'Cause Jesus rose for me
And he paid for all my sin.
Choc-late and jelly beans,
That's not what my Easter means
No bunny knows.
No bunny knows.

Easter eggs behind a tree
There to find for you and me.
It's lots of fun but just can't be
The reason for the season.

No bunny knows
That I can live again.
Because Jesus died
And he paid for my sin.
Choc-late and jelly beans
That's not what my Easter means.
No bunny knows.
Oh, no bunny knows.

SCENE 2: The Party

Jenna, Paige and Mike are wearing their costumes.

JENNA: Nice costume, Paige!

PAIGE: Thanks! I like your bunny suit! It's cute!

MIKE: Compliments are being taken for the blue Easter basket. Speak on...

PAIGE: Uh...nice tights, Mike.

MIKE: They're sweat pants!

PAIGE: Okay, nice sweatpants.

JENNA: Hey, here comes Ryan! And without a costume!

[Enter Ryan]

MIKE: Hey Ryan, why no costume? Or are you just a walking egghead? Ha!

RYAN: I came as myself—a person who is going to heaven someday because of what Jesus did.

ALL: Huh?

RYAN: To me, Easter isn't about bunnies and eggs. Those are neat things for Spring and all, but Easter is about Jesus being raised from the dead. After he was crucified, he was sealed in a tomb, but three days later he came back to life! And now we can live forever too.

Kids are silent, mouths dropped open.

JENNA: Now I feel like a complete dork….

MIKE: Yeah, me too.

PAIGE: Not me. I'm with Ryan. That's why I dressed like a lamb to commemorate Jesus, the sacrificed Lamb of God!

MIKE: The what? You are such a nerd.

PAIGE: Forgive the big words. Let me put it this way, I'm a lamb, because Jesus was the Lamb of God. You know.

MIKE: No, I don't know.

RYAN: What Paige means is that a long time ago, people had to sacrifice animals to take the punishment for their sins. That

way, the people could live. But God sent his Son, Jesus, to die for us.

PAIGE: Now God doesn't require animal sacrifices.

RYAN: We just believe that Jesus took our sins and we give him charge of our lives. And as for your costumes, guys, you shouldn't feel so bad. After all, bunnies are God's creation! Right, Jenna?

JENNA: Hey! Right!

PAIGE: And eggs can mean new life.

RYAN: Yeah, and Easter baskets are….

MIKE: (Anxiously.) Yeah? Yeah? Go on.

RYAN: And Easter baskets…

PAIGE: —can carry the eggs! How's that?

MIKE: That'll work!

The choir enters as if they're coming to the party. Kids find their positions on the risers or stage.

RYAN: Well let's join the party! But let's just remember what we're celebrating!

ALL: Okay!

RYAN: *(To the audience.)* Here's a favorite Easter song—page (give page number) in your hymnals! Stand and sing with us as we celebrate the resurrection of Jesus!

CONGREGATIONAL SONG: HE AROSE (Low in the Grave He Lay)

The End

Nobunny Knows

Words and Music by
Susan Parsons

No-bun-ny knows what
Eas-ter means to me, 'Cause Eas-ter means that Je-sus
died up-on a tree, and af-ter Je-sus died, up
from the grave he 'rose, That's a mys-ter-y, that
no bun-ny knows. No-bun-ny knows that

Special Occasions

At Christmas and Easter parents always look forward to seeing their tykes parade across the platform in colorful costumes. But other events in the church calendar may warrant a "prime time" presentation by your kids. You might not pull out all the stops for these occasions, but a nice little 15-minute presentation can help get a spiritual message across while giving the kids yet another opportunity to be useful and effective in ministry. In this chapter you'll find programs for

- *Epiphany*

- *Palm Sunday*

- *Missions*

- *Independence Day, and*

- *Thanksgiving.*

You can use these mini programs on Sunday morning to reinforce the pastor's message. Or present them at a special open house when parents can see what's going on in children's ministries at your church.

Epiphany

(intermediate)

On the Christian calendar, Epiphany (or the twelfth day of Christmas) is the celebration of the Magi finding the young child Jesus. According to tradition, these were the first Gentiles to worship him as the Christ.

This Epiphany presentation allows three of your budding young actors to shine! (Scripture doesn't mention how many wise men there were, but it does mention three gifts. That's why we usually make them three in number.) *The Epiphany Song* with three simple verses is sung to the simple tune of *Twinkle, Twinkle, Little Star*. You'll need three children to play the wise men.

Dress kids in wise men costumes as described in Chapter Three and give them richly wrapped gifts to carry. A golden box, a tall perfume vial and an ornate, bejeweled box would be wonderful.

- -

THE Pageant

The choir enters. The Magi enter to one side of the choir.

WISE MAN 1: Oh, my aching feet! How long have we been on the road?

WISE MAN 2: I've lost track.

WISE MAN 1: I wish I'd lose track of these blisters. Or just a few of my toes, maybe.

WISE MAN 2: You could try riding your camel more and walking less.

WISE MAN 1: Huh-uh. I have blisters other places too. *(rubs his backside)*

WISE MAN 2: Yeah? Well you're gonna give me *ear blisters* if you keep on complaining.

Wise Man 3 turns to them in a superior manner.

WISE MAN 3: My brothers—it is not seemly for wise men to bicker.

WISE MEN 1 & 2: *(Sheepishly.)* Sorry.

WISE MAN 3: Take comfort—we've nearly arrived. See—the star has stopped over that village.

WISE MAN 1: It has?

WISE MAN 2: It has!

WISE MAN 3: We shall worship the king this very night!

WISE MEN 1 & 2: *rap style*
Worshiping the king
Will be such a cool thing
With the gifts we have to bring.
Since we first saw the star
We have come so very far.
Now look—here we are!

Wise Men 1 and 2 give each other high fives. Wise Man 3 frowns at them and speaks in a haughty tone.

WISE MAN 3: Brothers!

WISE MEN 1 & 2: *(Sheepishly.)* Sorry.

WISE MAN 1: We're excited.

WISE MAN 2: Just a little.

WISE MAN 3: Indeed.

WISE MAN 1: It's good to be excited.

WISE MAN 2: I mean, this is the King of kings we're about to meet.

WISE MAN 3: Indeed.

WISE MAN 1: We'll assume a noble position.

WISE MAN 2: Watch.

They both mimic Wise Man 3's bearing. Wise Man 3 gets all excited and behaves like them.

WISE MAN 3: Cool!

They slap high fives all around, then assume a kingly bearing and process to join the choir.

CHOIR: THE EPIPHANY SONG
(Music on page 79–80.)

(Young children sing first verse.)
Twinkle, twinkle bright new star.
We are wise men from afar
Your great light has led us here
To the Christ child small and dear
Twinkle, twinkle great big star
We are wise men from afar

(Older kids join in; verse is in a minor key.)
See the Magi from the East
Worshiping the Prince of Peace,
Bowing to the child so small,
Who came to earth to save us all.
They gave gifts of riches rare
And thanked God who led them there.

(All kids together; major key again.)
People, people, see the light
God's great love is shining bright
Let his Word now be your guide
It will lead you to his side
People, people, see the light.
God's great love is shining bright.

Wise men step to the side again. The speak with solemn excitement.

WISE MAN 1: Can you believe it? God allowed us to find the Savior of the World. And we're not even Jews!

WISE MAN 2: We'll never be the same. The world will never be the same.

WISE MAN 3: His kingdom is for all people, for all time…for all the little children of the world!

Wise men lose their noble demeanor again and slap high fives.

WISE MEN: Cool!

Wise Men join the choir again and give high fives to several choir members. Choir sings joyfully, clapping and smiling.

SONG: JESUS LOVES
(Music on page 81)

Jesus loves the little children
All the children of the world.
Red and yellow black and white
They are precious in his sight.
Jesus loves the little children of the world.

Whether you're a Jew or Gentile
Jesus cares for you today.
If we call upon his name
He will save us all the same.
Jesus came to earth to take our sins away!

Choir and Wise Men Exit.

The End

Epiphany Song

Tune: Twinkle, Twinkle Little Star

Words by Susan D. Parsons

Twin kle twin - kle bright new star.

We are wise men from a - far. Your great light has brought us here.

To the Christ child small and dear. Twin - kle, twink - le bright new star.

We are wise men from a - far.

See the wise men from the East wor - ship - ping the Prince of Peace.

Bow - ing to the child so small who came to earth to save us all.

They gave gifts of rich-es rare, and thanked God who led them there.

Peo - ple, peo - ple see the light. God's great love is shi - ning bright.

Let His Word now be your guide. It will lead you to His side.

Peo - ple peo - ple see the light. God's great love is shi - ning bright.

Jesus Loves

Traditional
Melody

Second verse by
Susan D. Parsons

Mother's Day

(easy)

When we celebrate Mother's Day, we want to be careful not to limit the tribute to birth mothers. Include grandmothers, foster mothers and others who assume the role.

The song in this Mother's Day program was written for children with every conceivable family situation. It's a song of blessing from child to caregiver. The song, found on the CD titled "Lullabies from Potterfield Pond" (by Susan Parsons), would make a wonderful tribute to mothers, fathers, or anyone else with the responsibility of caring for one of God's little ones.

THE Skit

Choir enters. Arrange the five children with speaking parts on the edges or on the front row so they can step up to the mike and say their lines, then rejoin the choir. If you wish, have each child in the choir carry one or more carnations.

CHILD 1: Who gets up
in the middle of the night
To bring a drink of water,
or calm a little fright?

ALL: Mom does!

CHILD 2: Who makes us take a bath
and wash behind our ears?
Who give us encouragement
and wipes away our tears?

ALL: Mom does!

CHILD 3: Who scrubs the icky pans that no one else will touch?
Who gives us hugs and says, "I love you very much?"

ALL: Mom does!

CHILD 4: Who finds the dirt and dust that no one else can see?
Who makes us do our chores when we'd rather watch TV?

ALL: Mom does!

CHILD 5: Mom, you always give your best; your love, your smile, your smarts. So here's a little song for you that comes straight from our hearts.

SONG: GOD BLESS
(Music on page 84.)

(Available on the CD "Lullabies from Potterfield Pond" from Cook Communications Ministries, 800-708-5550.)

God bless those who care for me
I need them so much
I depend upon their care
With a loving touch
God bless those who lead my way
Help them do it like you say
This I ask tonight
So I can grow up right

If you would like to sing a second stanza, use these words:

God bless Mama, Daddy, too
Whether near or far
God bless Grandma, Grandpa, too
You know who they are.
Help them all to live your way
Help them do it like you say
Help them shine your light
So I can grow up right.

As the choir members leave to sit with their families, have them distribute flowers to each woman in the congregation. Have a helper or two in the back with extra flowers to assure no one is left out.

The End

God Bless

Words and Music by
Susan D. Parsons

Father's Day

(easy)

Intact families with both a mom and dad are a dwindling part of our society. So you'll want to take special care to celebrate dads and other father figures in your church. At the same time, you'll need to be sensitive to kids who don't have a dad at home. This father/son skit speaks to the needs of everyone by holding up our Heavenly Father as the ideal.

• •

THE SKit

Cast: Father, son (or daughter)

Scene: A garage or driveway. Dad has his toolbox and is trying to tighten the chain on his son's bike.

DAD: *(Tests the tension on the chain.)* I haven't got this quite right yet.

SON: But it's lots better than it was.

DAD: We're getting there. But I want you to be safe. We need to take a look a the brakes too.

SON: How do you know how to do all this stuff?

DAD: *(Laughing.)* I fake it!

SON: No you don't.

DAD: Well, I sort of figure it out as I go. My dad was really good at this kind of thing. I wish I had his talent.

SON: How old were you when Grandpa died?

DAD: (Age of son), just like you.

SON: It must have been hard growing up without a father.

DAD: I didn't.

SON: What do you mean? Grandma didn't get married again.

DAD: Nope, but I had a father just the same.

SON: I don't get it.

DAD: In fact, I still have my father. And I always will. He protects me, gives me good instruction, helps me prepare for the future, and provides for my family.

SON: Huh?

DAD: You have him to. And you'll still have him no matter what happens to me.

SON: Oh—I get it. You're talking about God the Father.

DAD: Smart boy! God is the Father of all nations. The Bible even tells us he's a father to the fatherless.

SON: Really? Where?

DAD: In Psalm 68. Go grab your Bible and check it out while I finish up here.

Son exits, then reenters with a Bible open to Psalm 68.
SON: I found it. "Sing to God, sing praise to his name, extol him who rides on the clouds—his name is the LORD—and rejoice before him. A father to the fatherless, a defender of widows, is God in his holy dwelling. God sets the lonely in families." That is so awesome! I didn't know the Bible said that.

DAD: It is pretty awesome.

SON: I have some friends who need to hear about this.

Dad hands him the finished bike.

DAD: Here. You can hop on your bike and go tell them!

Son hops on the bike and rides off shouting "Woohoo!" Dad picks up his tools and exits to the other side.

At this point, the kids' choir can sing a song about God the Father. You might want to use the familiar hymn "This is My Father's World" or "My Father's Eyes" by Gary Chapman.

The End

Independence Day
(easy)

The Fourth of July can be a difficult time for productions, since so many church members can be away on vacation. Learning lines can be nearly impossible! But even without a script of any kind, you can offer a special music number with your kids, and deck them out in Uncle Sam hats and Liberty crowns. Be sure that you line the kids up so that the hats do not obscure the children behind them. You

Figure 41

can place children in a single line across the stage, or use risers. Rehearse this in advance so you can offset any problems the hats may cause.

Choose one child to carry the American flag as the kids march up to the risers singing "You're a Grand Old Flag."

Afterward, they can sing the sweetly patriotic song, "American the Beautiful."

If these songs are not among your favorites, choose any of a number of songs that have sheet music or soundtrack tapes available. Some of these include "America the Beautiful," "Proud to Be an American," and "God Bless America." Check your local Christian bookstore for accompaniment tapes.

Figure 25

Missions
(easy)

It's always exciting to see the costumes of other lands during a missionary conference or special missions service. If possible, dress your children in the clothing of other countries and cultures for this presentation. Suggestions include:

Mexican

Boys—black pants, white shirts with open collars, colorful serapes.
Girls—white peasant blouses, colorful gathered skirts

Japanese

Girls—colorful kimonos, rubber thongs
Boys—white karate outfits, rubber thongs

Chinese

Girls and boys—jackets with mandarin collars, baggy pants

Northern European

Girls—embroidered blouses, dirndl skirts, braids
Boys—faux leather pants or shorts, fair isle sweaters

Scottish

Girls and boys—tartan plaid kilts and shoulder wraps, white shirts

Arab

Girls—billowy robes, head wraps
Boys—billowy robes, turbans

Indian

Girls—Bright silk-like fabrics wrapped sari-style
Boys—White nehru shirts and white trousers.

Native American

Girls—soft suede fringed skirts and blouses, moccasins, bead jewelry
Boys—soft suede fringed pants and loose shirts, bead and feather arm or headbands

African

Girls—brightly colored long cotton dresses, head wraps, hoop earrings
Boys—brightly colored woven cotton shirts

A simpler way to add international flair is to have kids make and carry small international flag. Do a search for international flags on your Internet browser and you'll find several excellent sites. Many clip art programs also have a very thorough international flag section.

THE PRESENTATION

Create spectacle by having kids march up the aisles with their costumes and flags. Use a CD of festival music, such as the Olympic theme as kids enter.

SONG: NOBODY'S TOLD THEM YET

(Music on page 90–91.)

Two verses appear in the sheet music. Teach children to sing all four verses with these words.

I'm glad I learned that Jesus
Paid for all my sin.
I'm glad I heard the message
And I let him in.

Chorus
Some people, they don't know
That Jesus paid the debt.
Some people, they don't know;
Nobody's told them yet.
I'm glad I have the Bible;

It tells me how God sees.
I'm glad that I have teachers
To make it real for me.
Chorus

Maybe when I'm done growing
I'll travel very far.
To where the kids don't know him.
I'll go where they are.
Chorus

We've got to let them know
That Jesus paid the debt.
One day if we make it happen,
Someone will tell them yet.
Chorus

The End

Nobody's Told Them Yet

Words and Music by
Susan D. Parsons

Go Forth

(Missions, intermediate)

Cast: Ling Mei, Kirby, Mr. Housenlot, Mrs. Lumbago, Selma Singlechick

Scene: *Outside in a typical American neighborhood. Ling Mei is sitting on a bench, looking very sad.*

THE SKIT

Kirby enters and sits beside her.

KIRBY: Hey, you're new in the neighborhood. What's the matter? Can I help?

LING MEI: My name is Ling Mei. I'm sad because my people have no hope.

KIRBY: No hope? What do you mean?

LING MEI: I am one of 5 million Nosu people in China. No one has told us about Jesus. I read about him in a book once, but I don't understand. And there's no one to explain.

KIRBY: Don't you have churches there?

LING MEI: No. We have no one to show us the way.

KIRBY: I've gotta do something about this right away. Don't worry. I'll find someone to help.

LING MEI: You will?

KIRBY: You bet. I'll start looking right now. There are lots of folks from my church right here in this neighborhood.

(Ling Mei exits. Mr. Housenlot enters carrying garden tools.]

KIRBY: Mr. Housenlot!

MR. HOUSENLOT: Hiya, Kirby!

KIRBY: I just met a friend who needs help.

MR. HOUSENLOT: Really? I'd be glad to help. Is it groceries? I could drop some off. Even give a ride to church. Where does your friend live?

KIRBY: In China.

MR. HOUSENLOT: China?

KIRBY: My friend's name is Ling Mei. Her people don't know about Jesus. Somebody needs to go share the good news. How about you, Mr. Housenlot?

MR. HOUSENLOT: Er, uh—me? Well, I...I can't , Kirby. I'm sort of tied down here with the house and job and family. Not to mention my prize roses. Takes years to grow them, you know. Find someone who's not so tied down.

Mr. Housenlot exits.

KIRBY: Hey—I oughta try Mrs. Lumbago! She's retired, and she's been teaching Sunday school for a long time. She'd be great!

(He knocks on a door. Mrs. Lumbago opens.]

MRS. LUMBAGO: Hello, Kirby.

KIRBY: Mrs. Lumbago, you're the best Sunday school teacher I ever had.

MRS. LUMBAGO: Why thank you, Kirby.

KIRBY: I found out about some other people who need to know about Jesus. They're in China. You up for a trip?

MRS. LUMBAGO: Not me, Kirby. I've done my part. It's time for me to put my feet up and watch TV. Oh—my favorite show is just coming on. Gotta go.

She shuts the door. Selma Singlechick enters.

KIRBY: Hm. There's Selma Singlechick! She's a college student. A perfect candidate!

SELMA: Hey there, Sweetie, whassup?

KIRBY: Do you like to travel?

SELMA: Sure. I went to Florida last spring break and it was like totally awesome.

KIRBY: Then maybe you'd like to go to China and talk to people about Jesus.

SELMA: No can do. I just met this really cool guy. I can't just go running off until I see how this relationship works out. Ooh— was that my cell phone? *(Answers her phone.)* Hello? Oh, hi David. Tonight? Oh, I'd love to!

Selma waves at Kirby as she exits, still speaking on the phone. Ming Lei enters.

MING LEI: Have you found anyone, Kirby?

KIRBY: This is harder than I thought. Everyone would have to give up something important, and no one seems willing. I'm sorry, but we'll keep trying, okay?

MING LEI: *reads from a Bible* Jesus said, "All authority in heaven and on earth has been given to me. Therefore go and make disciples of all nations, baptizing them in the name of the Father and of the Son and of the Holy Spirit and teaching them to obey everything I have commanded you. And surely I am with you always, to the very end of the age."

Kirby and Ming Lei exit.

The End

Palm Sunday
(easy)

Easter Sunday usually upstages Palm Sunday in terms of pageantry, and with just a week between them, it's not usually practical to plan for an elaborate Palm Sunday program. But Palm Sunday has a wonderful message that should be celebrated! And an EASY program makes it possible.

First, let's look at the message. It's more than one of people waving palm branches, saying, "Welcome to Jerusalem, Jesus!" These people were throwing down their coats for him—or rather, for his donkey—to tread upon, to shield him from the baseness of earth.

In Jesus' day garments were hard to come by. Further, they were important to one's personal identity. Shepherds wore shepherds' coats; rich persons wore cloaks of fine thread and extraordinary color. Priests wore very ornate garments. Pharisees and scribes had certain clothing that identified them according to their roles in society. Many people only had one or two sets of clothing—none but the rich had full closets like today. So when they threw down their coats, they, in effect, yielded their very selves to Jesus. It was a humble act of complete, heartfelt worship and praise.

To truly worship God, we lay down who and what we are, just as the people did in Jesus' day.

Give each child a palm branch. Order them in advance from a florist, or make them from green construction paper and paint stirrers, or from green poster board. In a pinch, use lengths of green curling ribbon attached to a plastic ring, or even crepe paper streamers.

If possible, let your children wear Bibletime clothing. For this production, let some of the girls wear floral crowns with their costumes; others should wear typical Bibletime scarves. Lead the children from the back of the sanctuary behind the two criers.

CRIER 1: He's coming! He's almost here!

CRIER 2: Everyone get ready to sing his praises!

Play the intro to the chorus. Choir enters and surrounds the congregation as they sing a wave their palm branches.

SONG: HOSANNA MARCH
(Music on page 95.)

Hosanna! Jesus has come!
Hosanna! He is the king!
Hosanna! Come give him glory!
Hosanna! Join us and sing!
(Repeat, encourage the audience to sing.)

Have your accompanist slow the chorus and transition into the hymn "Crown Him with Many Crowns" in the same key.

While the kids and congregation sing the first verse, have the children with the Bibletime headpieces spread their head coverings in front of the pulpit or a cross, then kneel around them, as before their King. This illustration of humility can be very effective on a spiritual level. As the pastor assumes leadership of the service, the children can disperse to sit with their families.

Hosanna March

Words and Music by
Susan D. Parsons

SAN- NA! Je- sus has come! HO- SAN- NA! He is the King! HO- SAN- NA! Give him the glo- ry! HO- SAN- NA! Join us and sing! Join us and sing!

Thanksgiving
(easy)

Let's talk turkey here. During Thanksgiving break, many churches already are in the midst of intense rehearsals for their Christmas programs. Parents are busy; kids are busy. This means, you need an easy, no muss, no fuss Thanksgiving program you can present on a Sunday morning. And here it is!

Figure 27

Although not absolutely necessary, it would help to have pilgrims' hats—tall, wide brimmed black hats with buckles for the boys, and white Pilgrim caps for the girls (fig. 27). Those representing Native Americans should wear feathers (fig. 42). Dutch friends should wear Pilgrim garb as well.

Before the program, have a stash of vegetables and fruits hidden around the platform. Pumpkins, corn and gourds are especially appropriate. And a fake turkey, if you can find one!

Figure 42

THE SKIT

Cast: English Christians, Dutch Christians, Native Americans

Children dressed as Dutch Christians wait offstage to the left. Native Americans wait offstage to the right. Two or more children representing English Christians wait at the back.

NARRATOR: Long ago in England, certain Christians wanted church to be more meaningful.

English Christians enter from the back. They kneel to pray.

They thought church had lost its meaning. It didn't challenge them to live as Jesus taught. They wanted to find a better way to worship God and live for him. So they left England and went to Holland.

Dutch Christians enter. The children who were praying get up and join the Dutch.

Not everyone was pleased with this group of Christians. They finally realized that in order to be truly free to worship God, they would need to make the dangerous journey to a the New World—the land that would become America, land of the free.

Kids form a single row facing the pulpit and start "rowing." Odd numbers should row on the right; evens on the left.

It was a treacherous voyage through storms and rain, seasickness and dwindling supplies. After weeks of sailing on cramped, wooden ships, these pilgrims finally reached their new homeland.

Native Americans gather at the left. Pilgrims mime getting out of the boat and excitedly meet the Native Americans.

They met new friends—Native Americans who generously shared their food with the fair-skinned strangers. Together, people of these very different cultures gathered for a special feast.

The actors find the vegetables and fruits hidden around the platform and place them in a pile in the center. They gather in a circle around the food and raise their hands and heads to heaven in thanks.

Now at home in a new land across the sea, the pilgrims gave thanks to God for providing for all their needs.

Kids assemble as a choir and sing a song of thanks, such as "We Gather Together," "Faith of our Fathers," "Give Thanks" or any other relevant song of your choosing.

Thanksgiving Painting Parade
(easy)

During the weeks before Thanksgiving, set up an art workshop where children can paint pictures that represent things they're thankful for. Encourage the children to make their paintings large and bright. Have them practice telling in one or two sentences what they're thankful for and why.

For the program, place the paintings on an easel at the front of the sanctuary.

Have children line up in the order their paintings will appear. Have your accompanist play soft music as the children come to the microphone one by one to tell about their paintings. After they speak, have them find their assigned places in the choir.

THE PRESENTATION

SONG: WE GIVE THANKS
(Music on page 99.)

Oh Father of Love,
We give thanks this day
For the food on our table
And the freedom to pray.

For the warmth of our homes
And the sun up above;
For the warmth of our hearts when
We think of your love!

Oh Father of Love,
May our thanks be sincere
Not only this day,
But each day of the year!

After the song, have the children file out of the sanctuary or find their places with their parents.

The End

We Give Thanks

Words and Music by
Susan D. Parsons

O   Fath-   er   of   love,   We
For the   warmth of   our   homes,   and the
O   Fath-   er   of   love,   may our

give   thanks   this   day,   For the   food   on   our
sun   up   a-   bove,   For the   warmth in   our
thanks be   a-sin-   cere,   Not -   on-   ly   this

ta-   bles   and the   free-   dom   to   pray.
hearts   when   we   think   of   your   love!
day,   but   each   day   of   the   year!

Stagecraft and Special Effects

Nothing grabs and holds an audience like spectacle—great sets and unusual sights and sounds. And there are a whole host of great, fun-to-do special effects you can add to your shows.

Backdrops

You can create backdrops in a number of ways. Let's start with the traditional theater flat.

Theater flats are typically eight feet tall and five feet wide. They consist of a frame of two-by-fours braced at the corners with triangles of plywood. These braces have to be on the back of the frame. You'll also need to brace the flat in the center with a 2"x4" that extends across the width. This can be a five-foot strip nailed on the outside, or you can remove four inches from the length and nail it between the two eight-foot strips. Be careful that it doesn't protrude in the front of the flat.

Figure 33

Otherwise, it will mar your canvas.

You can make the flat stand alone by adding two-by-fours, three feet long, to the bottom of the flat. Let these "feet" stick out one foot in front and two in back. Using heavy-duty screws, secure one of these strips to the bottom of the flat (see illustration on next page).

Stretch theater muslin tightly over the

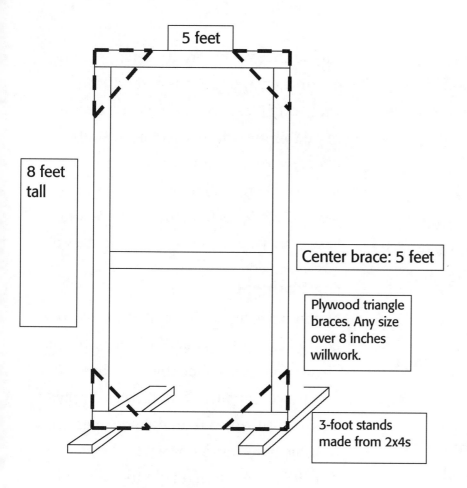

5 feet

8 feet tall

Center brace: 5 feet

Plywood triangle braces. Any size over 8 inches willwork.

3-foot stands made from 2x4s

frame of 2″x4″ wood to which you can nail it. It may be possible to use narrower cuts of wood; just be sure it is braced so that it won't twist or "squeehaw."

PAINT

You absolutely have to use matte or flat paint for backdrops. Semi-gloss and glossy paint will produce glare and make it hard to see the actors.

BACKDROP PATTERNS

The patterns on pages 108–111 provide an outline for basic backdrops you'll use again and again. Photocopy them onto transparencies, then project them onto flats or sheets and you'll be well on your way to creating some great sets!

SPECIAL EFFECTS

Special Sounds

Sound effects can really perk up your show! For example, the sounds of thunder and rain would add a lot to the story of Noah's Ark! Many music stores have sound effect CDs, and many are available on the Internet. But if you must, you can make

frame and staple it to the sides. "Paint" the muslin with an equal mixture of white glue and water and let it dry. When the muslin dries, it stretches tightly so that wrinkles are removed, and the surface is ready for paint! When several flats are braced together, you can paint a veritable mural to serve as your background!

Another thing you can do is use large sheets of cardboard. Companies that ship their product nearly always have quantities of cardboard in large sizes, and many are willing to donate to a church production. If you paint cardboard, it *will* warp! For this reason, it is imperative that you first build a your own! The kids in your youth group would love producing sound effects for you, and it gives them an important role in the program's pre-production. Just look at these ideas:

- Cars going by on a busy street. Be sure to tape long enough to get good background for your entire show. Keep the volume low so the background noise isn't overpowering.

- Thunder and rain. It's fun to record a storm. Stay safe and dry by setting the microphone on a window sill or covered porch and just let it roll.

- Crying babies. A visit to the church nursery will probably suffice!

Sounds of kids in a school hallway. You'll need to get permission from the school administration.

Animal noises. What a great excuse for a field trip to a farm! A little "mooing" and "baaing" add wonderful atmosphere to a manger scene.

Electronic keyboards are a great source of recorded sound effects. Assign someone to explore the sounds on keyboards owned by your church or by members who might be willing to lend their keyboards for your production.

Strobe Lights

Strobe lights (high-speed flashing lights) can be effective in certain scenes, such as dream scenes, depictions of destruction, wild party life, and others. Please bear in mind this important safety note: strobe lights have been known to trigger epileptic seizures when flash rates exceed five per second! While such occurrences are rare, it's best to set your strobe light at a safe level.

Fog Machines

Nothing creates an ethereal mood like a light blanket of fog hanging low in the air. Linseed-oil smoke machines can be purchased or rented from theater supply houses. Be warned that fog machines can be difficult to control. You need lots of practice to maintain a light fog. You don't want huge cumulus clouds of smoke unless your script calls for it. You can find less complex fog machines for sale at party stores for very reasonable prices.

Dry Ice

Dry ice is frozen carbon dioxide, or CO^2, which is a gas. You can get dry ice from ice dealers, meat packing companies and other places where cold transport is common. A large block of dry ice in a dishpan of water will bubble and emit a lazy white cloud. You may want to build cardboard flanges around your pan to concentrate the cloud and give it direction. Just experiment with it until you get the desired effect. But remember—the bigger the slab of dry ice (submerged in water), the more smoke you'll get. And don't touch the dry ice with bare hands. You can actually get burned! Another note: don't let babies crawl around in the mist or let anyone lie down in it, no matter how fun it looks. It does not support life and a person, especially little ones, could asphyxiate if left to breathe it for very long.

The Dream Screen

One of the most effective ways to produce "dreams" or angelic "visitations" is with the use of a cheesecloth scrim and back lighting. Using a scrim as your backdrop curtain, your backdrop can be opaque when lit from the front. But when it's lit from behind, the audience can suddenly see through the wall and into another dimension! I used this technique to show Jesus being raised from the dead during a play. We built an opaque tomb of plywood and PVC pipe, but the round stone that formed the doorway was made of thin theatre muslin painted like a rock with very thin paint—just enough to stain the fabric without clogging the mesh. When Jesus rose from the dead, a bright flood light was turned on inside the tomb and Jesus, in white, could be seen rising up from the slab. The audience squealed in surprise and the applause was thunderous!

You can also use this ethereal effect to create a dream slightly behind your character. Just make sure you've constructed a dream cell that's opaque on all sides (even the top!) except the muslin front.

To create the best effect, you need to choose the right kind of theater muslin—a thin cheesecloth. Be careful not to choose cheesecloth that's too thin (a threadcount that's too low), or you'll be able to see through it before the back light surprise! And be sure to tell the actors inside to be perfectly still until the light comes on. Sometimes movement can still be seen through the best of scrims.

When you use this "dream cloth," the houselights and frontlights should be down. It creates a super-cool spectacle!

FUN PROPS

Rock Seats

Rock seats add a fun 3-D effect to your sets (fig. 43). And they're the perfect "perch" for a wise man, Mary, a shepherd, a contemporary school child, or even a creature from the wild!

You'll need:

- A milk crate
- Lots of masking tape
- Newspaper

Figure 43

Figure 44

- Big mixing bowl
- Flour and water
- Black and white paint with wide (2") brush
- Piece of cardboard (wider than the crate)

This is fun and easy! Place the crate, open side down, on the sheet of cardboard (see fig. 44). The cardboard should be a few inches wider than the crate. The bigger, the better, in this case.

Run masking tape from the bottom of the cardboard to the top of the crate—the tape will not have anything to stick to between the top and bottom, but there's a purpose for it (see fig. 45).

After running several strands of tape around the crate and the cardboard base, crumple balls of newspaper as shown (see fig. 46) and stick them into the spaces created by the tape strands. As much as possible, try to camouflage the cube shape

Figure 45

Figure 46

Figure 47

the edges down flat. Apply at least two layers.

Your rock will have to dry for at least 24 hours before painting. It should feel hard and hollow, not spongy or soft. Mix a little black paint into a cup of white and stir until you get a nice medium gray color. Then take a paintbrush and paint all over the rock. Be sure to cover all print, but you

Figure 48

by stuffing irregular balls of newspaper at seat level, and allow them to slope down.

When the areas are well stuffed, make your flour paste by mixing half a five-pound bag of all-purpose flour with warm water—just enough to give it the consistency of pancake batter. Here's a test to see whether it's just right: Dip your hand into the batter. When you bring it out, it should stick to the top of your hand as shown in figure 47.

Next, tear strips of newspaper. They should be between two and four inches wide, but size really doesn't matter here. Dip the strips in the batter and remove the excess between your fingers. Drape the strips over the seat of the crate first. Lay them in various directions, for strength, and to prevent a pattern. Then begin draping strips from the seat area and down the slopes and crags formed by your crumpled newspaper (see fig. 48). Again, crisscross your strips in haphazard order, smoothing

don't have to worry about some white showing through. It actually adds to the look of texture! When you're done with the gray, take your brush, dip it in some black, blot it, and run the brush over some of the bumps and lines. It will define them and give your rock more character! The only mistake you can make is to create anything that resembles a brush stroke or line. Blobs, smears, streaks and smudges are welcome here!

Tree Stump Seats

A tree stump seat adds a nice "touch of nature" to your set.

You'll Need:

- A large plastic bucket (industrial-size paint buckets work well)
- Heavy muslin or an old sheet
- Flour paste in a bucket
- Black, white, and tan paint
- Crumpled newspaper

This is one of the easiest props you could make, but it can be messy, so do it in a garage or basement with a drop cloth. Start with making the flour paste by mixing half a five-pound bag of all-purpose flour with warm water—just enough to give it the consistency of pancake batter.

Cut an old cotton sheet or muslin in a large circle—about five feet in diameter. It doesn't have to be a perfect circle, so don't spend a lot of time measuring! Soak the circle in the flour paste. Wring it out so that it doesn't drip. Then, drape the cloth over the upside-down bucket. Smooth the top, then smooth the sides, welcoming those wrinkles as bark texture! At the bottom, pull the fabric away from the bucket to form roots angling out to the sides. Crumple newspaper and stuff it under these roots to give them some form. Only make a few roots, just like a big oak tree!

Let the stump dry for a couple of days. Then paint it very dark brown all over (use dark brown paint with some black added for a nice deep brown/black). When that dries, use a large brush with charcoal gray paint (black with a little white) and brush over the top of the bark. Don't fill in the creases—let the brown/black remain there. Paint the seat with tan, allowing a one-inch rim of brown/black. Use a darker brown to paint rings in the seat, like an irregular "target". There! You've got a sturdy stump for your actors to sit on!

Fireplace

Fireplaces with stand-still flames made of orange cardboard are boring! You can made an ultra-realistic campfire or fireplace that's easy and fun to see!

Let's start with the fire.

You'll Need:

- Orange silk (*not* satin!) or very light nylon or other synthetic that "floats"
- A small, battery-operated fan (or electric, as long as it's very small, five inches or so)
- A small electric light (15-watt bulb or less—such as a bare nightlight) . If you can find an orange or yellow light, all the better!
- A small cardboard box, such as a shoe box

Firewood

Cut strips of silk in different widths and lengths (only about six inches, but you can start longer and experiment), with pointed tips. These will be tongues of flame. Tape or tie the "flames" to the grill on the fan so that when the fan turns on, the flames blow outward.

Cut a large hole in the shoebox, so that you can lay the fan on top of it, facing upward, without it having any obstruction of air circulation. Cut holes in the sides of the box to allow airflow. Lay the fan over the top hole and turn it on. The flames should lick straight upward. If not, they're too heavy, either from being the wrong fabric or just being too long. Experiment until you get just the right look.

Pile firewood around the box to camouflage it. Place the light on the floor, in front of the fan.

Turn on the fan and the light, and turn the houselights down. You'll want to make S'mores or grab a guitar and sing campfire songs!

For a realistic fireplace, use a large cardboard appliance box. Cut the box down so that it's only about two feet in depth. Turn it on its side and cut a neat, square hole in the bottom This is the fireplace opening. You'll need to leave a "frame" of about eight inches on three sides. The bottom will be flush with the floor.

Paint the frame to look like stones or bricks, and place your campfire setup inside! Cozy!

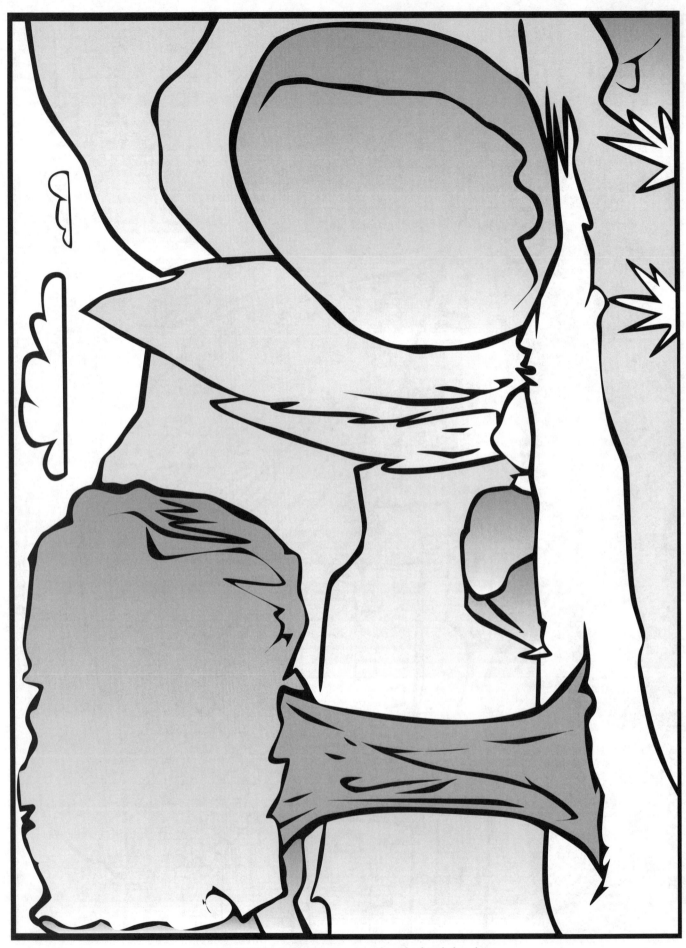